Get Your Woman On!

Embracing Beauty, Grace & the Power of Women

Presented by
Kimber Lim

Yinspire Media

Presented by: Kimber Lim
Producer: Ruby Yeh
Editorial Director: AJ Harper
Print Management: Book Lab
Cover Design: Pearl Planet Design
Book Design & Typesetting: Chinook Design, Inc.

info@yinspiremedia.com
www.YinspireMedia.com

ISBN-13: 978-0-9819708-3-7

Printed in the United States of America

Contents

CONTENTS

CONTENTS

CONTENTS

Kimber Kabell Lim

Introduction

I magine a love that you can call your own: A love that sees you, feels you, and reflects that image back to you. A love that saturates every fiber, every cell in you so fully that you can barely contain your excitement at the contagious burst of creativity that starts to percolate into a rapid bubbling fountain, a dazzling cascade of endless potential. Such a love will stand all tests of time. It will, without fail, guide you in discernment and keep you out of harm's way.

The stories in this book are grounded in a love that begins with ourselves and transforms us, giving us the courage to take another step, another breath. That love is quiet in the way it so naturally flows to care for a loved one, lend a helping hand to a stranger, give a smile and a hug. It is loud when we see others suffering with no means to protect themselves.

Do you yearn to be unreasonable and define success on your own terms? Have you ever wondered at your power as a woman and seen how the world so needs you, needs us?

Perhaps we must give *ourselves* a helping hand first. Perhaps, because our value is so important, we must correct our own course and ask for guidance from those who have a teaching, a message, a wisdom for us that will dissolve whatever barriers are in our path. In this book, women who have overcome abuse, injury, discrimination share their triumphs. Women who have looked fearlessly deep within themselves to find their core beliefs tell the story of love and faith acting in their lives.

Why would we as women expect anyone else to build the world we want, rather than create it for ourselves? Our stories show how, when we are living truly and fearlessly from our truth, miracles happen.

As you read this book, you'll be in awe of the adventure of unfolding. You may pinch yourself with glee as the seemingly impossible becomes reality. We hope our stories, our visions, spread the seeds of hope, inspiration and sincere benevolence, that they bring forth a world in which women are honored, nurtured, respected and cherished.

Our stories illustrate the capacity that each woman has to simply care: Care for ourselves, those we love, those strangers we pass on the street, those around the world to whom we extend our hearts in times of crisis and in the celebration of victories large and small. Through that caring, we women have the capacity to change the world.

We have collaborated in this compilation of messages from women around the world, from various walks of life and of all ages, who share their life experiences and the wisdom they have wrested from them. We wrote them for you.

No matter where we are in the cycle of life—no matter what any of our circumstances, challenges, triumphs—we have far more in common then we have in differences. In our stories, you may find yourself. You will know that you are not alone and discover how you can move forward in your life. Our stories represent hope, an opportunity to promote and assist each other.

We extend a connection, sharing how we took action, how we shifted our perspectives, how we benefit others. Our stories from the heart are your story as well. For, like all the women in our stories, you matter, you matter to me and you matter to the world.

Dr. Jean Shinoda Bolen
Transforming Ourselves, Changing the World

Y ou have an assignment…
      Only you can recognize when an assignment has your
name on it. You may not know what it is yet; you may have just
received an inkling; or you may be standing on the threshold of a
new beginning.

Only you can say, "This is meaningful to me;" or know that you
are deeply drawn to be with others who care about the same thing;
or sense that your assignment will require your being authentic,
creative or trusting of your destiny. A soul-level assignment is
motivated by love—even when it appears as an outrage, when what
you love is being harmed. It is a challenge to live your values.

Whatever your age, your talents, or your stage in life, your whole-
hearted response to an assignment will lead to transformative
change. It may be through taking the first small step, or daring
a huge life-altering leap. It will take you into uncharted and deep
territory in yourself, and open you to a bigger outer world.

You won't know where this response will lead you. For example,
I think of Vivienne Verdon-Roe. She was a schoolteacher in the
Midwest when she saw *The Last Epidemic,* a powerful documentary
on the nuclear arms race, and was stirred to activism. One step
at a time, beginning with an inner conviction, she answered
each assignment as it presented itself, until one day she became a

documentary filmmaker herself. Within just a few years, she was accepting an Oscar for her film, *Women—For America, for the World.* Where will your assignment—your adventure—take you?

Some time ago, I discovered my own personal assignment: I am a message carrier. The result was a book: *Urgent Message from Mother: Gather the Women, Save the World.*

I believe that humanity is at a crossroads. We hang in the balance between two possible futures—a future of war, inequity and destruction of natural resources, or one of abundance, peace and prosperity. I believe that critical-mass, grassroots activism transforms consciousness, which in turn changes history. What

> *When enough of us heed the call and come together in spiritually-centered circles of support, we can change the world.*

women do in the next few decades will determine the fate of life on this beautiful, abundant planet. While it may seem implausible, it certainly is possible for women to steer our planet toward a healthy, peaceful and sustainable future. When enough of us heed the call and come together in spiritually-centered circles of support, we can change the world.

There is ample precedent in our recent history for this kind of grassroots change. The women's suffrage movement started with a group of five friends. They were scorned and sometimes mocked by men, but they kept going and growing until women got the vote. The civil rights movement, the women's movement, the gay rights movement and the campaign for nuclear disarmament all relied on this principle: Small groups grow to bring about a substantive shift in global consciousness, leading to new policies, new laws, new alliances of peace and understanding.

How do small groups lead to big change? It's simply the function of critical mass. When enough people see things in a new way, or change their behavior and it reaches what writer Malcolm Gladwell calls the tipping point, suddenly what was mocked and resisted

4

becomes what everyone assumes to be so: "Of course, women have the right to vote." "Global warming is real." Real change can start very small. It can start with you.

The "hundredth monkey" allegory, written by anthropologist Ken Keyes, outlined this principle, which in turn inspired the activists who helped bring about the end of the nuclear arms race between the superpowers. Keyes reported how new behavior by a young female monkey spread through her colony and then was observed in other monkeys, islands away, with no apparent direct influence.

The allegory was based upon theoretical biologist Rupert Sheldrake's morphic field theory and consistent with C.G. Jung's theory of the Collective Unconscious. Through these, or by geometrical progression, new ideas and behaviors begin small and

> How do small groups lead
> to big change? It's simply the
> function of critical mass.

become infectious until a critical number of people accept them. You may not be the first monkey, but you may be the sixteenth, or the seventy-fifth, or even the ninety-ninth. The unit that can change the world now is a circle with a sacred center.

Circles of women have long been a powerful medium for healing, and have relied on an egalitarian principle rather than one of hierarchy. In such circles we are safe; we are equal; we are nurtured; and we are empowered. In a circle, we can discover our assignments and speak the truth of our callings for the first time, even if just in whispers, at first. In a circle, the resolve to take on our assignments is strengthened.

Certain principles help a women's circle to function well, and to be a healthy and vibrant. First there must be a sacred core to the circle, which is tapped into with silence for contemplation, meditation or prayer. Trust depends upon confidentiality, and the intention to listen with compassion, not judgment. This creates the safe, nurturing space where we are free to question, reveal, share and grow.

I'm involved in an exciting idea called the Millionth Circle Initiative. "The millionth circle," like the "hundredth monkey," is the metaphoric one that tips the scales. It's the one that will bring the feminine principles of caretaking and circle gatherings into the culture. When enough women come together in enough circles, this powerful, positive tipping point will be reached. A proliferation of circles with a spiritual center becomes a worldwide healing force.

The Millionth Circle brings feminine values of relationship, nurturing and interdependency into a global culture in which

A proliferation of circles with a spiritual center becomes a worldwide healing force.

hierarchy, conflict, competition, power over others and exploitation of the earth's resources are the dominant values. It is an idea whose time has come.

I am also looking forward to and working to bring about the Fifth United Nations World Conference on Women, with a projected date of 2015. Imagine thousands of women coming together from all over the world to further our positive agenda for humanity, sharing the inspiration of their stories and ideas that work. Imagine millions of women in villages, neighborhoods and big city venues tuning in through technology; imagine millions of circles of women taking on assignments. Imagine transformation.

The Dalai Lama was talking about us when he said, "The world will be saved by Western women." The Dalai Lama was talking about you. We are the ones with the freedom, the education, and the resources to effect real change in the world. And women's issues are really, at the core, humanity's issues.

A world that is safe for children will not breed terrorists; a world that is safe for women is a world where children are safe. Creating a safe world, a beautiful world, a peaceful world, begins with you courageously embracing your assignment, and then faithfully following the path to see it fulfilled.

When I reflect on the seed for individual transformation, I think it comes from two different places. Sometimes the need for change, for moving away from hurt or pain, brings about the transformative process. Other times it comes through a kind of epiphany, an awakening. Then you are in a truly sacred space—the threshold between what you were and what you are becoming.

Planet Earth and humanity are on such a threshold today. Through the Internet, we are connected in ways we never have been before. New possibilities are with us that we've never encountered before. And when all women can use these tools, these resources, to work together—well, that could really create results. It begins with you, with your unique and important assignment. Declare it. Embrace it. Champion it. In doing so, you will transform the world.

Jean Shinoda Bolen, MD, is a psychiatrist, a Jungian analyst, and an internationally known author and speaker who draws from spiritual, feminist, Jungian, medical and personal wellsprings of experience. She is the author of The Tao of Psychology, Goddesses in Everywoman, Gods in Everyman, Ring of Power, Crossing to Avalon, Close to the Bone, The Millionth Circle, Goddesses in Older Women, Crones Don't Whine and Urgent Message from Mother. Her new book, Like a Tree: How Trees, Women, and Tree People Can Save the Planet, was released on Earth Day 2011.

Jean is a Distinguished Life Fellow of the American Psychiatric Association and a former clinical professor of psychiatry at the University of California at San Francisco, and is a past board member of the Ms. Foundation for Women and the International Transpersonal Association. She has been featured in two acclaimed documentaries, the Academy-Award winning anti-nuclear-proliferation film Women— For America, For the World, and the Canadian Film Board's Goddess Remembered. For guidelines on creating your own women's circle, please visit www.MillionthCircle.org. Connect with Jean at www. JeanShinodaBolen.com.

Kimber Kabell Lim

This Is a Love Story

The night is caressingly warm, but the ocean off Hannalei Bay is chilly tonight. I sort through my scuba-diving bag and decide on my dive booties and a scuba diving skin. I need the protection of the skin anyway. The barnacles can be extremely painful, poisonous, and night diving presents a lot of dangers. The tides can sweep you out to sea; tiger sharks roam the perimeter in search of a meal and often float into the shallowest places.

Until tonight, I've never had a hobby. *How is it that I've made it to fifty and never had time for a hobby? I've been so focused on business, family, friends, making a difference in the world, always saying, "I'll get to that, I'll get to me later."* I laugh softly, wondering if maybe I should take up something simpler, less dangerous, like painting or ancestral research—anything but lobster diving. But I want an adventure, just for the pure joy of it, as well as to slow down, pay attention and learn something about myself.

With the moon half full, the black velvet canopy of night is darker than usual. After checking out several beaches, my trusty dive buddy, Jay, and I had settled on diving off of a remote part of the Kauai coast. I look up at the endless cascade of dancing, twinkling stars and it seems I could reach right up to the void and and touch the light.

But the illumination I found was actually from my miner's headlamp. Jay gathers our gear and basket in tow, we venture into the pitch black, cool water.

It seems the tide has drawn out for a quarter of a mile. We've no choice but to navigate, *sans* fin, the slimy moss, treacherous barnacles and rocky reefs on the ocean floor. Finally the ocean shallows give way to open water and we dive. I surface to the roar of the waves.

Twenty feet away Jay yells, "Watch out for the riptide." As much as I want an adventure, as much as I want to discover the woman I am without rules, without the high pressured life-style I have created, I certainly don't want to be swept out to sea! I don't know of anyone who has lived through that. When the tide surges, I manage to stay upright, the water pulling, twisting, churning all around me. It goes on for an eternity, and I surprise myself: I won't succumb into the abyss.

As we dive deeper, the ocean gives way to endless crevices hiding night creatures. I remember Jay's warning: "If you see only one lobster antenna, that means an eel is likely behind him." Eels bite and I wouldn't want to lose any precious appendage. I'm distracted from my fear by the mesmerizing cacophony of underwater nightlife. In the depth of open water, we sight a pair of lobsters. Grabbing briskly to avoid their claws, we drop the catch into our metal basket. We drift the basket a good twenty feet away because lobster is live food (bait) and if a tiger shark picks up the scent of prey, I don't want to be someone's dinner or share mine.

We're headed for a secret turtle reef, home to at least forty feet of multiple ledges filled with sleeping turtles and a bounty of lobsters. But not tonight! The sea is rough and visibility is so poor, we signal to return to shore. I can't see more than two feet in front of me and as we drift apart I can't find my dive buddy. I am on my own, alone.

The incoming tide pummels me backward, knocking me off my feet onto a shallow reef. With bare hands, I reach for something to grab and realize I forgot my dive gloves! I know to keep my hands tucked close to my body. I know I could grab a poisonous porcupine-like barnacle that can temporarily paralyze me, but I have to avoid being pulled into the riptide.

I am tossed relentlessly across the jagged reef. My head aches from hitting the lava rocks; the cuts in my hands and face sting in the salty water. Reaching out I find a perch and grab on. Now steady, I see nothing but darkness. The only sound is the night jungle and ocean. I'm alone, in the ocean, in the dark, thousands of miles away from who I've known myself to be.

My stepmother's voice bubbles up from memory repeating the mantra she always used. "Just fine." People would ask, "How are you?" and even when it was so far from true it was laughable, she would offer up a strained smile and say, "Just fine."

Just fine brought me to the brink of burnout and now has me on my knees as the next wave hits. *Just fine* was a polite-ism for

> I'm alone, in the ocean, in the dark, thousands of miles away from who I've known myself to be.

I'm scared, angry, frustrated, tired… any truly passionate response. Alone in the dark water I am so far from fine, and I see now: Just fine is binding me to a familiar ideal that was slowly distancing me from myself and my spirit. I look up at the swirl of constellations in the sky and I know that my spirit shines as brightly.

The next wave gets my attention and clearly, I can no longer live a life of "just fine" or "good enough." I hear my inner voice say, *You aren't fine, yell for HELP.* I scream and Jay spots me, signaling to drift towards shore.

Profound calm permeates me and I know I'll guide myself to shore, over the reefs, holding onto my center. I call upon my inner wisdom, power and truth. Back on my beach I find my friend. He's not surprised in my ability to trust my gut and brave the forces of nature.

Nonetheless, I am shaking like a leaf being in the cold water. Gathering sticks, dry grass and coconut shells, we build a fire on the beach. In the warmth of its flame, staring at the sky, I breathe the night air, in tune with the life force of the surrounding ocean and jungle.

I make a prayer of gratitude: Please let me know and never forget the beauty of life and self-trust. Let me feel and live the richness of now with power and grace as woman. No matter when, no matter where, let me align in partnership with the divine; I have what it takes to have an authentic, truly successful and wealthy life in accord with my values and terms. At some point, I had become so skillful at the masquerade, I simply forgot the vulnerable, tender heart behind the mask.

I came to Kauai to get a break, to unplug. I stayed to heal. I spent months reviewing my life, sometimes being gentle, sometimes being headstrong and fierce. I'd make a fire on the beach, no one for miles, and pray with gratitude for all of the blessings I experienced. I climbed lava cliffs without trails in search of myself

> *At some point, I had become so skillful at the masquerade I simply forgot the vulnerable, tender heart behind the mask.*

and my courage. I began to dismantle the beliefs, the masks I'd worn since childhood, breaking apart the mold of what I was told a woman should "be, act, speak (not)." I pulled away the layers and uncovered decades of truth: ideas, broken hearts, bold musings, unpopular opinions and a tender spirit I didn't even know existed beneath my well-practiced camouflage.

I know this seems like an adventure story, but it's not. This is a love story. I have become my own heart's desire. I say to myself, *I will not abandon you again, Kimber, I will attend to your needs now!* On this island, away from the demands of *the life I had built,* that had left me unfulfilled, I found my truth: That simply being a woman was the greatest gift I could behold or give. I found a love and appreciation of self, a oneness with spirit and the nature of all things. I found my voice there on the shores of the bay, and in the jungle; I found true beauty and grace, I can count on this woman I have become.

I had never known, or even dared to dream, that such sweetness of spirit existed. I thought it came from others, status or possessions, rather than life force itself. In a misunderstanding of service and generosity, I had forgotten my dreams and put discovering my happiness on hold. In speaking my heart truth, I

I know this seems like an adventure story, but it's not. This is a love story.

can hear and honor that of others. And, in living fully in tandem with God, Spirit, and the Divine, I feel safe, loved and shielded. I don't need to hide my heart any longer, or pretend I don't have one. I'm rebuilding a new one.

I treasure the simple life and moments no longer wasted. And, I know there are other men and women out there who want the same.

When we live in our own truth, beauty and grace, women are powerful beyond measure. Even when the tide threatens to pull us away from our true selves, even when we (or those around us), try to label us or confine us, even when we hold ourselves back from our own greatness, we will always find our way back to shore if we have the courage to begin. Take my hand.

In her twenty-five years as a business coach, speaker and entrepreneur, Kimber Kabell Lim has shared her formula for having a wildly successful life and wildly profitable business with more than a hundred thousand entrepreneurs and CEOs globally. These collaborations have created billions of dollars in revenue while making a difference. To fulfill her mission to help women create "grace, power and beauty in all areas of life, health and wealth," she founded GetYourWomanOn.com and to champion men and women in conscious business, she founded TransformationalBusiness.com. Kimber co-authored the bestselling book, The Law of Business Attraction. Connect with Kimber at www. GetYourWomanOn.com and www.TransformationalBusiness.com.

Sandra Yancey
Women Soaring Past the $1 Million Mark

When I was a little girl, I thought my mom had her groceries delivered. It started when I was five years old, after my father died. Every couple of weeks two men in suits would show up at our house with several grocery bags. I loved it because it was the only time my mom would let me sit on the counter.

From my perch, I reached into the bags and handed my mom the goodies for her to fill up our nearly empty cupboards. Included in each delivery were loaves of bread, peeking out from the tops of the bags. I had heard the term "breadwinner," and so I assumed the men had *won* the groceries. I was in my late teens before I learned that the gentlemen who delivered our groceries were church volunteers from the Society of St. Vincent de Paul, an organization that distributes food to poor people.

We didn't *seem* poor. My mom was so proud—she never let us see her struggle, never let on that she needed help, so it came as a huge surprise to me. Suddenly, I looked at her—*really* looked at her. And I saw a very private woman living a life of quiet desperation. What if she had asked people to help her start a new life after my father died? What if, when she came up against seemingly insurmountable obstacles, my mom had a circle to lean on, to help her find a solution, to lift her up?

I knew that, if my mom had just set aside her pride and asked for real, life-altering help, she would have lived a very different life—an expansive life filled with opportunities, accomplishment and joy.

My mother is not an educated woman, but she is a wise woman nonetheless. She always said, "Step on me. My job as your mom is to raise you up, so you'll do better." She *knew* it was possible for me to live a different life than the one she was living, and she wanted more for me. Her words bored into my heart, giving me a purpose and the courage to pursue a bigger dream. *Step on me. Let me lift you up. Do better.*

"I *will* live a different life, a better life," I vowed to myself, to my future husband, to my friends, to anyone who would listen. And I did do better—much better. I went to college, graduated, and went on to earn a master's and a post-graduate degree. I married and cared for my young children full-time, and when they went on to school I built a successful career as a corporate consultant.

> *When you have a philosophy of giving first and sharing always, the universe gives you exactly what you need when you need it most.*

Through the years I kept my vow front and center, honoring my mother's wishes for me to "do better" and my own desire to live a different life from hers. But there was more, so much more for me to do. Though I didn't realize it at the time, my vow was also a promise to the millions of entrepreneurs I would one day connect, educate and empower through my company, eWomenNetwork. *As I climb, I will lift YOU up.*

When I launched eWomenNetwork in 1999, I yearned to create an environment where women who were very serious about monetizing their passions could come together for the purpose of sharing information, knowledge, contacts, resources and leads. With the help of my husband Kym and our amazing team, we've built a caring, supportive environment focused on giving first and sharing always, helping our global network of women (and men) garner the necessary knowledge to start, run and grow their businesses. Together, we lift each other as we climb. *Step on me. Let me lift you up. Do better.*

When you have a philosophy of giving first and sharing always, the universe gives you exactly what you need when you need it most. When the energy you put out into the world is "let me help you, let me inform you, let me help you because it's the right thing to do," the universe sends that energy back to you when you least expect it. This philosophy is the foundation on which eWomenNetwork was built, and for the women in our network, it is at the heart of every "unrealistic" goal achieved and every "impossible" dream fulfilled.

Over the past eleven years, we have realized my initial vision for eWomenNetwork—women all over the world, too many to count, are launching and growing wildly successful businesses, creating much-needed jobs and pursuing their dreams with a steel will made stronger by the knowledge and nurturance of our network. Although there is more exciting work to do, I am so moved every time one of the women in our network shares her triumphant story of breakthrough success.

Yet none of this was a surprise to me, frankly. I knew my dream of transforming traditional self-focused ways of networking into an other-focused approach would work particularly well for women. We are, by nature, very caring and helpful. It's part of our DNA, and is reinforced by example—by our mothers.

What did surprise me were the things we, as women, need to work on. Chief among them is our unwillingness to ask for help. We exhaust ourselves multitasking, and then wear the bags under our eyes like a badge of honor. It's as if somewhere along the line we drank some sort of Kool-Aid and bought into the belief that "no one can do it quite like me, so I might as well do it myself!" While that may be admirable, and in some cases necessary— particularly in the early stages of a business—the attitude just can't be sustained as a company grows. This is where we get ourselves into a real pickle. We need to *do better*.

Just because you're great at something doesn't necessarily mean it's great *for you*. The truth of the matter is, you have to focus on the things that really make the cash register ring. We must behave as true CEOs—Chief Executive Officers, not Chiefs of Everything. It's really easy to get caught in that multitasking trap and avoid asking for what you need, when you need it.

I have to remind myself of this every day. I ask myself, "Hey you, who are you telling women to ask for help when you're not asking for the help *you* need?" The thing is, I get so close to it, and end up falling victim to the same things I implore other women to avoid. I'm not an expert; I'm a student of life. And sometimes I have to take my own medicine. We all get caught up in the business

> *We exhaust ourselves multi-tasking, and then wear the bags under our eyes like a badge of honor.*

of life, trying to keep all the plates spinning on the poles: be a good daughter, wife, mother, businesswoman, sister, colleague, friend. We forget that we need help, that we really do need each other.

My next big goal is to empower women to break the $1 million annual revenue mark. Only two percent of women entrepreneurs ever make $1 million in annual revenue, and I'm convinced this is partly due to our just-let-me-do-it attitude. It's our Achilles' heel, the "fatal flaw" that keeps us from the mountaintop. We may be great at lifting others as we climb, but we still have to work on asking for our own leg up.

There is a word I can't stand: *fine*. Women use it over and over again, and rarely mean it. "I'm fine," "Everything's fine, thanks," "Never mind, I'm fine, I'll just do it myself." Pay attention to the way men talk. I find that, generally, men don't use the word *fine*. Men are better at saying, "This is a problem I have that I don't know how to answer," or, "This is where I need some help." Men are better at reaching out and seeking assistance. I think that the more we create environments where women have permission to solicit help, the more we will see a profound transformation among women entrepreneurs.

Looking back on my childhood, I understand now that my mom was a woman who needed more than just groceries, more than just a donation, more than just a helping hand to get through the month. My mom needed a way up and out of the poverty she could not escape after my father died. She needed other women

We all get caught up in the business of life, trying to keep all the plates spinning on the poles: be a good daughter, wife, mother, businesswoman, sister, colleague, friend. We forget that we need help, that we really do need each other.

(and men) who would lift *her* up, connect her with opportunities, help her develop her talents and abilities and create a vision for her life so that *she could do better.* My mom needed a network, but she never really had one because she was too ashamed of her circumstances to ask for the help she needed.

Really, she's a microcosm of all women. We all have our reasons for avoiding asking for the help we need, but if we want more women breaking the $1 million mark—if YOU are going to break the $1 million mark—we must find a way to say, "Help me." I've always said that my five favorite words are, "How can I help you?" As we look to transform ourselves, our businesses, our communities, our country and our world, we must add five new words to our list of favorites: "Would you help me, please?"

Our moms are our role models in different ways. My mom modeled the things I wanted for my life, and the things I wanted to rise up and move away from. Today, I have my own twenty-year-old daughter, and I find myself saying, "Here, step on me. Let me lift you up so you can do better." And I remind her to always ask for help, even when she wants to do it on her own. In modeling both her grandmother and her mother, my daughter will not only climb to great heights, she will soar.

Sandra Yancey is a networking expert who teaches others how to create relationships that harness great dividends. She is the founder and CEO of eWomenNetwork, the number one resource for connecting and promoting women and their businesses worldwide. Ranked by Business Women's Network as the best online community for women business owners and professionals in North America, eWomenNetwork. com is the most visited women's business website on the worldwide web, receiving more than two-hundred-thousand hits daily. Through eWomenNetwork, Sandra recently launched the Success Institute, giving entrepreneurs unprecedented access to a whole new set of knowledge from thought leaders and authors. For women, by women, the Success Institute shares the best of the best, helping women scale their businesses.

Sandra is the recipient of numerous national business awards, including the 2005 Entrepreneur Star award from Business Women's Network and Microsoft. She hosts the top-rated eWomenNetwork Radio Show, which broadcasts out of Dallas on the highest-ranked ABC affiliate, 820 WBAP. Sandra has been profiled in hundreds of newspaper and magazine articles throughout North America and is recognized as one of the leading authorities on the topics of networking and relationship-building.

Sandra is the author of the book, Relationship Networking: The Art of Turning Contacts Into Connections, *and was featured in* Chicken Soup for the Entrepreneur's Soul. *Connect with Sandra at www.eWomenNetwork.com.*

Dr. Emma Jean Thompson

Believe and Be Blessed

L ate one night, when I was about eleven weeks pregnant, I began bleeding. As the bleeding became steadier and more profuse, my husband and I rushed to the hospital. "You've passed tissue," the examining doctor told me, coldly. "You've lost the baby, and your life will be in jeopardy if I do not do a D&C procedure immediately." As I hesitated, I could see him getting angrier and more impatient. "You have to do it now," he said.

But I wanted to give this person, my child, a chance to live. "Isn't there something I can do to save my baby's life?" I pleaded with the doctor. "Isn't there some test I could take to show me whether my baby is still alive before you scrape my womb?"

The veins stood out on his neck. "No! There is no test. It's too early. You have to do this—otherwise you could walk out into that hallway and drop dead."

My husband and I had been married for twelve years and were waiting to have a child. In my ministry, I had prayed for so many women who had been told they could not conceive; I'd seen miracle after miracle occur as they got pregnant and gave birth. It had not yet happened for me. But the Lord had told me that I too would conceive and have a child one day, and I had trusted in His message and had looked forward to it for all these years. When we finally discovered I was pregnant, we were overjoyed.

The doctor did not want to hear my story. "You'll just have to start all over again," he shot back. And, frustrated, he stalked out of the room. My husband and I held each other's hands tightly and prayed.

I closed my eyes and remembered how, on an Easter Sunday morning long ago when I was ten years old, my father had abandoned our family. That day, I had a revelation from the Lord that although my earthly father had abandoned me, my Heavenly Father, God, would never leave or forsake me. Since then, my whole life, I had trusted in the guidance of the Lord. For years I had been used by God prophetically to minister to others and to give them messages from the Lord. And I also helped them to know how to hear God. Now, as I always did, I listened for the voice of the Lord to counsel me in making my decision.

And immediately I sensed—I knew—*I will not have this procedure tonight.* Though I was still bleeding heavily, I would leave this doctor's office and seek the advice of a new doctor in the morning. My husband and I looked into each other's eyes and

> *But I wanted to give this person, my child, a chance to live.*

squeezed each other's hands, nodding. The doctor walked back into the room with a piece of paper in his hand. I said firmly, "Thank you for your help and advice, but I am not going to have the procedure. I am going to wait and see what my other options are."

He blew up. "You have to sign this document," he shouted, shoving the paper at me, "to show that I have told you that you are putting your life in jeopardy." I signed it. "You can leave," he said, and walked out of the room.

My husband went to pull our car up to the hospital entrance, and since I was weak and still bleeding heavily, the nurse, Myra—God forever bless Myra—helped me get dressed and wheeled me to the car. "You go home and rest," she said, kindly. "Doctors are not God." It was a long, long drive home that night as I thought of everything the doctor had said to frighten me into the DNC. But for all his intimidation, I thought, *No—I believe God. And even if the baby is not there, God is faithful, and I will praise Him and give Him glory.*

Early the next morning, I visited a new doctor. "You're still bleeding," he told me after the examination, "but your uterus is very thick, which is a good sign. And your cervix is closed, which

> *But for all his intimidation, I thought, No—I believe God. And even if the baby is not there, God is faithful, and I will praise Him and give Him glory.*

is also a good sign. We'll do some lab tests and give you a call." The wait felt interminable. When he finally called back, he said, "I want to tell you that you are carrying a very viable eleven-week-old baby. We don't know why you're bleeding, but we can't find anything wrong, and the baby is fine." I hung up the phone and cried, elated and relieved. *We have received our miracle!* The bleeding subsided a short while later.

Several months into my pregnancy, I was diagnosed with gestational diabetes. The doctors prescribed continuous insulin. I'd seen countless miracles of healing from just about every ailment you can name. I'd also seen people get locked into medication as a way of life. I didn't want to take the insulin, though the doctors warned me that if I didn't, my baby could be oversized, diabetic or have a host of other problems. She could even be stillborn. They were very compassionate and concerned; they knew how much I wanted this baby. *But I want the Lord to touch my body. I want to receive a miracle and be healed.*

So I waited. And I watched others in our church receive miracles—like Shawn, a young man who had suffered from crippling rheumatoid arthritis since he was a child. One Sunday, while he slowly limped to the front of the church, I sensed that he would receive God's healing. And indeed, he laid down his cane. "I feel like running!" he cried. "Run!" we told him, and he raced down the aisle with a glorious smile on his face.

Then, one Sunday, God again touched me. I received my miracle that night, when I checked my blood sugar levels and saw that they were even better than they would have been with the insulin shots. "These are the facts," I told the doctors, again and again. "Even if you don't believe it is God's grace at work, there is no reason for me to be on insulin with these blood sugar levels." They shook their heads.

But at last, as Sherah was being born, the doctors said, "You knew what you were talking about! The baby's fine! The baby's

> *Making room for Jesus transforms your life in so many wonderful ways.*

fine!" What a blessing—even the doctors were glorifying God. To hear them say, "The God you serve is real," filled me with joy. And I couldn't wait to see my baby girl, the greatest blessing of all.

When the nurse brought her to me, and I looked into her beautiful eyes, I said, "Thank you, Jesus." How beautiful to see her, after our long journey. She was not just my child, a perfect being; she represented God's faithfulness. Even if she had not lived, I would have praised Him. But what a blessing that she was alive, and He allowed me to hold her in my arms! Hallelujah. I gave her the name Sherah, "builder for God." Today, Sherah is twenty-five, healthy, a graduate student and a wonderful, powerful woman of God.

We do believe in the value of doctors and medicine—but first, we acknowledge the Lord and pray. This is where I found the right guidance. Sherah survived and thrived through God's blessings and miracles.

My decisions were not made haphazardly. In showing Jesus my love and trust in His glory, I was making room for Jesus to show me *His* love. And if I had not made room for Jesus, I might never have had my daughter.

Making room for Jesus transforms your life in so many wonderful ways. When you make room for Jesus by believing in Him in your heart and expressing God's love, you enjoy a more fulfilled and happier life. You find a peace, trust and exuberance that will lift you even in difficult times and challenging situations. "Who is he that overcometh the world, but he that believeth that Jesus is the Son of God?" (Colossians 1:12.) The first and most crucial step in the journey is to believe in your heart that Jesus is Lord and confess with your mouth that God the Father raised Jesus from the dead. Receiving Jesus Christ into your heart as your Lord and Savior brings a precious peace and an indescribable joy.

But absolutely everyone, regardless of faith, can demonstrate God's wonderful unconditional love—the love he expressed when he gave His Son—by doing something kind for someone, every day. It can be as small as writing a card or being generous with your smiles, or as large as caring for a friend in crisis.

Making room for Jesus also encompasses prayer, and taking time, in our very busy lives, to acknowledge the Lord. When Jesus was born, he was placed in a manger because there was no room for him at the inn. Let us not relegate Jesus to a modern-day manger, but rather, express God's love by making room for Jesus in the inns of our hearts, our minds and our plans, and by showing His love to everyone around us.

However you decide to make room for Jesus and express His love, know that He works miracles, and that God truly loves you. In all my years of faith and ministry, I have seen—and been touched by—more such miracles than I can count. Through belief, we are truly blessed.

Dr. Emma Jean Thompson is internationally esteemed as a speaker, #1 bestselling author, motion picture producer and trusted advisor serving leaders in ministry, business, education, entertainment and other arenas. She and her teams have been featured in various media including *CNN, CSPAN,* Time Magazine, USA Today, The Brian Tracy Show *and the* Michael Gerber Show, *with scheduled appearances on ABC, CBS and NBC. She is the founder and CEO of MakeRoom4Jesus. com for which the Dedication Celebration was sponsored and hosted by dear family friends Dr. Nido R. and Mariana Qubein at High Point University.*

Through "Wisdom Truths" of the Holy Bible and documented success stories, Dr. Emma Jean helps you—as thousands of others have been helped—to "Make Room for Jesus" in your everyday life and, as a result, more than double your income, your free time and your peace of mind as you joyfully fulfill your God-given life purpose. As an end-time Prophet and Apostle of God and Jesus Christ, Dr. Emma Jean helps YOU profit and prosper and be in health even as YOUR soul prospers (IIIJohn2-Holy Bible). Her "Purpose Passion" is to "Cause young people and adults to be blessed in every way in this earthly life AND to be ready for the coming of Jesus Christ and Judgment Day." Connect with Dr. Emma Jean at www.DrEmmaJean.com.

Andrea Herz Payne
Be Bold on Behalf of Others

My husband Hunter pointed to a table across the room. "Look, Jay Leno is sitting right over there. We should go talk to him about Darfur." It was a Saturday night, the end of a very long week and I was exhausted. *The last thing I want to do is interrupt Jay Leno and his wife like some crazed fan,* I thought. "It's a really good idea, but I'm sure they'd like to be left alone," I said. We went on with our dinner, but when Jay got up to leave, Hunter took my hand, looked into my eyes, and said, "Andrea, who are we doing this for?"

Before I knew it, I was up out of my seat, out the restaurant door and chasing after them into the parking lot, shouting, "Mr. Leno! Mr. Leno!" When I caught up with them, words tumbled out of my mouth: "My name is Andrea. We're working on bringing awareness to the genocide in Darfur, and I would just like to share it with you." I expected a cursory "We'll look into it, thanks," or, "Uh, I'm very busy right now," but instead Jay and his wife Mavis talked to us for fifteen minutes!

As we spoke, I could see the wheels turning in Jay's mind, and he said, almost to himself, "Clooney is coming on the show in a couple of days. He's involved with the Darfur issue." *Clooney? As in George Clooney?* Mavis suggested I send information to her office, and that was it. We said our goodbyes. I thought, *You just chased Jay Leno through a parking lot, Andrea. Wow!*

Later that week, when George Clooney was a guest on *The Tonight Show,* Jay asked him about Darfur. When George moved on to other subjects, Jay kept bringing George back to the subject of Darfur. His last question touched my heart. He asked George, "What can people do for Darfur?" I wondered, *Did we do that? Did we make that happen, just because we set aside our fears?* If I hadn't stood up and chased him down, we would have missed an amazing opportunity to make a difference.

I reflected on the last few years, to the beginning of our journey as humanitarian activists. It began in 2004, after the Indian Ocean earthquake caused the tsunami that hit Southeast Asia, and we still had no word from our friends Jeanne, Tony and their four small children who were vacationing in Phuket, Thailand. Sitting at our kitchen table, Hunter read aloud news accounts of the devastation. *They would have been near the beaches,* I speculated, remembering my last trip to Phuket with their family. *What if they're injured? Or dead? What if Jeanne and Tony are separated from the children?* We were helpless, waiting for news, overwhelmed by the reports from media and relief organizations. The tsunami killed hundreds of thousands, and left millions homeless. How could our friends survive this catastrophe unscathed?

Then it came—an email from Jeanne letting us know they were all right. Breathing a huge sigh of relief, I scoured the email for details, noting that "Even though we are okay, nearby buildings and beaches were decimated, babies were ripped from their mother's arms, and thousands are hurt or dead." We were deeply moved to read that our friends and other hotel residents had banded together, commandeering the hotel vans to deliver food and supplies wherever help was needed. It was incredible receiving a firsthand report from the front lines of this huge tragedy and, inspired by our friends' humanitarian efforts, we wondered what we could do from ten thousand miles away that would make a difference.

A week later, I had a "light bulb" moment. Hunter, a musician and composer, had been making plans to market his new record. I proposed, "Why don't you put together a CD compilation of songs donated by our indie music friends and raise money for tsunami relief?" Hunter loved the idea, and after some thought, it got much, much bigger. "Hey, if I were Sting or Paul McCartney or some other famous musician, maybe I'd want to donate a song, too," he said. *Sting or Paul McCartney?* It wasn't just big; it was bold—and completely crazy for two artists like ourselves with limited connections and no experience in international aid.

What happened next seemed like pure magic, or providence, or both. Hunter shared his idea with the guys at his twice-weekly basketball game. One of them knew the head of a prestigious music label who, when he heard about the compilation, gave us the pick of any track in their music catalogue. We chose "Here

> *It wasn't just big; it was bold—
> and completely crazy for two artists like
> ourselves with limited connections and no
> experience in international aid.*

We Go Again" by Ray Charles and Norah Jones, which had won a Grammy award the previous year, and were off and running. Just months later we had commitments for sixteen tracks donated by major artists including Eric Clapton, Bonnie Raitt, Maroon 5, James Taylor, Avril Lavigne, and yes, even Paul McCartney!

Right about the time we figured out how to license and publish the music, we heard that the William J. Clinton Foundation and UNICEF had all the money they needed for tsunami relief. We were astonished. *How can this be? Do they really have all they need to build back these leveled communities?* "This doesn't make sense," I said. Hunter responded, "You're right. We have to go to Southeast Asia and see for ourselves."

We traveled to remote areas where we were able to see the true scope of the devastation. A year and a half later, hundreds of thousands of people still lived in tents and mud, cobbling together a life with no jobs and little food, living on hope. We also met truly heroic people working for small, local organizations nobody in the United States knew about, organizations dedicated to developing and implementing real, lasting solutions for the survivors of this epic disaster. We came back even more inspired than we had been when we first read Jeanne's email. But the tsunami was long out of the news cycle; the media had moved on to other, more recent crises. We asked ourselves, *Will anyone buy the CD when it comes out? Will anyone care?*

During this time, we got involved with other NGOs (non-governmental organizations, or nonprofits) working on important issues. We heard reports from friends in New Orleans that, two years after Hurricane Katrina, conditions were still awful. We were puzzled: *Why isn't the media reporting on this?* We also met people working in Africa, and heard about a genocide of astounding

> We will be the voice of those forgotten.

proportions taking place in a region of Sudan called Darfur. This was a three-year-old conflict, and still another story the media wasn't covering. Our hearts were opening. We were becoming activists. With each day we became more informed, our inner fire grew, compelling us to be bold on behalf of others.

A passionate email I wrote about Darfur ended up in the hands of National Basketball Association player Ira Newble, who was studying the issue. Hunter and I immediately realized that if we could get the sports community talking about Darfur, the general public might listen. Film company Participant Media heard about our outreach and asked us to help them with the campaign for their documentary, *Darfur Now.*

By this time, we were used to being bold and going for the big "asks." So we decided to jump in, and inspired many well-known athletes to do public service announcements (PSAs): Steve Nash, Grant Hill, Olympian Rafer Johnson and others. It was in acting on behalf of others that we had accomplished so much. And because we had lots of practice being bold, I was able to jump out of my seat that evening and chase down the legend of late night television and ask him for his help, something I *never* would have done before. In service to others, I had started to become the woman I'd always hoped to be.

In the fall of 2007, the CD almost finished, we went to New York City to meet with Robert Piper, who had worked in President Clinton's United Nations Office of the Special Envoy for Tsunami Relief before it closed. He told us stories of survivors still living in Internally Displaced Persons camps, of houses in disrepair, about

> Do not let your fears get in
> the way of being great!

the lack of early tsunami warning systems and other serious issues that desperately needed aid and attention. Hunter and I had the answer to our question: "Will anyone care?" As we left Mr. Piper's office, we said, almost in unison, "This is exactly the point! We think no one cares about the tsunami and nobody will buy the CD because it's not in the news anymore—and that's precisely why we have to do it."

These largely forgotten people and issues gave us our mission. We decided to name the CD *Aid Still Required*. Later, after Participant Media completed their campaign, Kobe Bryant and five Los Angeles Lakers came back to us, expressing interest in doing PSAs on our behalf for Darfur. "We can't waste this opportunity. Their PSAs could change lives," I said. We agreed we had to get their message out. Sitting at our kitchen table, just as we had three years before, we made a vow: *We will be the voice of those forgotten.*

We knew that many organizations still working on the ground needed funding. We knew these issues needed someone to care enough to raise awareness. We knew these largely forgotten people—the survivors—still needed just as much help as they needed the day the cameras arrived to film the devastation. "We'll do the PSAs with Kobe and the Lakers," I affirmed. "We'll make *our* organization the voice." And so Aid Still Required, named for our CD, our mission, was born.

Today, we work full-time to fulfill the mission of Aid Still Required: to bring awareness to forgotten issues and to support sustainable projects in the field to restore lives in devastated regions. I'm still amazed by what we've accomplished so far. From those first kitchen table moments, when we didn't have a clue or a plan, to the good work we do now, we have always said, "Why not?" We didn't set out to become activists, but in embracing the opportunity to make a difference, we are becoming more than we ever imagined.

Working on a daily basis to alleviate suffering, I forget about the magnitude of the project, the sheer "impossibility" of it all. I've trained myself to think of "no" as "not yet," to see that "no" is just the beginning of a conversation, and to stay engaged in the pursuit of "yes" until I get it—or something better. There were and still are times when I feel discouraged, or afraid to approach someone, and I think, *My "smallness" is not worthy of the task at hand.* But then I remember our mission, the people, the possibility of making a *real* difference, and I tell myself, *Do not let your fears get in the way of being great!*

The beauty of being bold for others is, the more you do it, the stronger the muscle becomes. And soon, you can be bold on behalf of yourself, too. I've seen that the chance of something incredible happening is so much greater than any of my concerns; and that chance gets me over the edge of my fear. The same is true for you. I'm a "regular" person who is finding boldness in myself. You can, too. We are all powerful—we all have the capacity to make a difference. So be bold. Keep asking. And ask again. Go for the big, awesome, seemingly impossible goal. Do the crazy thing, the thing no one else is doing. Do it because you are passionate about it. Do it because you can. Do it because, together, we have the power to change the world.

Andrea Herz Payne is the co-founder and Chairman of the Board for Aid Still Required, a not-for-profit organization dedicated to helping people rebuild their lives in the aftermath of natural disasters and humanitarian crises by raising awareness about "forgotten" issues and by partnering with local organizations to create and support sustainable solutions. Connect with Andrea at www.AidStillRequired. org.

Sherrin Ross Ingram

The Essence of Strategy: Getting to the Heart of Getting Things Done

My husband and I had grand hopes for our first child. We had been married for thirteen years when we had our son, Michael. I imagined our boy attending the school for gifted children down the street from our house by age three and helping me pick out stocks and options at six. My husband was a pro basketball player for years, so he envisioned Michael's bright athletic future.

When our son began reading single words at just over a year old, I thought, "Oh, he's a genius!" and left it at that. But earlier, I'd noticed how Michael completely avoided eye contact and wasn't quick to respond to our voices. Even though he was reading full sentences by the time he was two, I was convinced that something was just not right.

His doctor gave us the usual speeches: "Boys develop slower." "Everybody develops in his own time—you shouldn't compare him to other children." But before Michael came, I was very focused on my career as an attorney and business strategist and hadn't spent much time around children. I had *no one* to compare him to.

If I had not enrolled Michael in toddler classes, I would have continued to live with my suspicions longer. But when I saw him with other kids his age, the differences were undeniable. He was completely uninterested in, and disengaged from, the activities. In his music class, all the other children sat in a circle on their mothers' laps, clapping along with the guitar. Michael just wanted to stare at the flags outside the window or touch the instruments. Rather than hold him on my lap, I ran around the room after him.

Kids that age play side-by-side, rather than together. Still, it was clear that Michael had a total lack of interest in other children (or adults). Most people thought he was just a very quiet kid. But I often felt my heart sink as I watched him stare for long periods of time, in a kind of fog, at the moving blades of the ceiling fan or at the spinning wheels on his toy cars and trains. These were his favorite activities. He would have stared for hours if I let him. Even snapping my fingers or clapping my hands near his face sometimes wouldn't lift him from his trance.

When we got the preliminary diagnosis of autism, Michael was two and a half years old. At the time, it felt like my life had ended. Hearing the word "autism" in the same sentence as my son's name was devastating. I felt a deep fear for his future (and ours), mixed with feelings of shock, grief, anger, embarrassment, helplessness and defeat.

I had tried so hard to do everything perfectly—always preparing beautiful organic meals (and eating them during pregnancy, too); choosing not to vaccinate my son; and having a family member care for him at my home when I decided to go back to work.

But this carefully planned strategy did not insulate us from pain, disappointment and dashed expectations. I felt such a sense of loss.

I immediately launched into warrior mode, something I was quite accustomed to doing from my days as a litigation attorney with a large Chicago law firm. I aggressively pursued a variety of therapies and allopathic supports in my effort to cure (actually, the word I used was "kill") autism. I didn't see it as a balancing process—I saw it as something that just needed to be fixed. Once it was fixed, I imagined, Michael would just wake up the next morning and no longer be autistic.

But soon, I recognized that I was exhausting myself with the stress of this approach. It really made me question myself: me, the lifelong strategist. So I started studying healing modalities from all over the world and really working on myself.

When I began to meditate every day and get in tune with my inner wisdom, fascinating insights emerged. I recognized that I needed to deal with my own baggage. I had approached the situation from a place of fear. The result had been an undermining focus that limited my perspective. Basically, I needed to change the way I defined and developed strategy. I had to figure out my

> *That is the essence of strategy:*
> *providing foundational support to the*
> *underlying factors that drive*
> *achievement of a goal.*

purpose and my real goals in order to decide where my focus should be. And when I realized that my purpose is to create a happy, healthy life for my son in a way that truly respects who he is, I changed my focus from curing/killing autism to *facilitating health and well-being*. I began using multiple healing methods and aggressively improved his diet.

When I became focused on health and well-being, my fear— and even autism—were naturally excluded. I have found that focusing on health and well-being leads you to consciously and deliberately provide support to your whole body and to your life as a whole rather than provide support to just one organ or set of symptoms. So often, we make the huge assumption that there will be health or quality of life in the absence of a particular condition or set of symptoms. It is now clear to me that unless you resolve the underlying imbalances that caused the condition or symptoms, some other (seemingly unrelated) condition or symptoms will come along and take its place. Since the precise underlying imbalances are not always known, it makes sense to "cover all bases" by providing comprehensive foundational support.

For example, my previous focus on "killing" autism resulted in efforts to "fix" Michael's brain and gut. I quickly learned that focusing on "killing" a condition gives energy to the condition (it eventually permeates every area of your life) and keeps you in the eternal state of managing symptoms. My new focus gives energy to the life-supporting factors that naturally seek to maintain the balance needed to prevent or eliminate autism, fear or any other undesired condition. In other words, providing foundational

> *The circumstances are not as important as your courageous commitment to something big and worthy.*

support for the whole body, mind and spirit naturally (albeit slowly) achieves more major goals. That is the essence of strategy: providing foundational support to the underlying factors that drive achievement of a goal.

Because of this experience with my son, my Actionable Strategic Planning® process now includes developing specific strategic support for the core underlying factors that drive achievement and satisfaction: clarity of purpose, commitment and the right focus.

Have you ever wondered how it is that so many people can fulfill their goals and still be so unsatisfied with their million bucks or with whatever else was atop their to-do list? They didn't get to the heart of their purpose and uncover what they are actually committed to achieving; as a result, they were focused on the wrong things. That's also why many find it difficult to consistently stick to a particular strategy or goal. A wrong focus based on a superficial purpose will fizzle.

The essence of strategy is not about how you plan to accomplish a goal; the essence of strategy is about identifying, understanding and fully supporting the core underlying factors that drive achievement. The circumstances are not as important as your courageous commitment to something big and worthy.

Approaching autism with fear was always about me wanting to bring Michael into *my* world, because my world saw no value in his world. But autism has taught me that if you're trying to get someone to see your point of view, you don't make that happen by discrediting *his* world. I had to join Michael *where he was*. If he wanted to watch a ceiling fan spin, I'd watch a ceiling fan spin, too. Suddenly, to my shock, he would look up at me as if to say, "What do we do next?" In fear, I had been trying to distract him, to pry him out of his reality and make him fit into mine. But when I let go of that fear, we connected.

Can you imagine being in your world, in the middle of doing something you love, and here's someone jumping up in your face, saying, "Hey! Look at me! Notice me! Buy from me! Do business with me!" You'd avoid that person too, because that's not the way we work. You want someone to take the time to know you and your true needs; you want her to value you as a human being *before* she

> *You are good right where you are,*
> *and it will only get better from here,*
> *with the right focus.*

offers you a "solution." Once I no longer feared autism or needed to conquer it, I started being more involved in what Michael was interested in. And then, conversely, he took interest in what I was doing. I could never have reached that place with him if I had not relinquished my focus on curing/killing autism and chosen a strategy based on connecting with him and facilitating health and well-being.

Understanding the essence of strategy and getting to the heart of getting things done in your own life isn't complicated, but it may require a shift in your focus.

The first step is to understand that wherever you are in the journey, hope is not lost. Your current expectations are only one way to focus and live out your circumstances. Don't get so hung up on what is "right" or "wrong" in your life. Just know that where you are is a *good* thing because it has the potential to give you clarity about your purpose, true desires and your driving forces for change. You can accelerate your progress if you develop the right focus and don't look at your current situation through fear's eyes. You are good right where you are, and it will only get better from here, with the right focus.

Whether it's personal or business goals, getting to the heart of your driving forces requires knowing who you are and incorporating that truth into your strategies. Spend some quality time in prayer and meditation and really listen for answers: Who do you want to be and why? What do you want to create and why? What's driving your desire for change? When your commitment is to something great, your courage is fierce.

Now that I've silenced my fear, I no longer feel a sense of loss. It is replaced by heartfelt gratitude for everything Michael is. I know that my unwavering commitment to his overall health and well-being and the energy I project toward him—accepting him for who he is, letting him explore and letting his own brand of genius take him wherever it is he is meant to go—has been healing for both of us: My strategy development skills have been sharpened, tested and elevated to new heights. I am properly focused, energized and, most important, *enjoying the ride* in all areas of my life.

Michael is out of the fog and totally engaged with the world. You can't do anything these days without him wanting to know, "What are you doing? What's going on? Why are you doing that?" And *that* is beautiful. *That* is success to me.

Sherrin Ross Ingram, known widely as "America's Leading Power Strategist," is CEO of the International Center for Strategic Planning and Chief Strategist for The Strategic Thinker's Mastermind. She is also an attorney, founder of The Foundation for Real Nutrition and Sustainable Living, a bestselling author and a popular motivational keynote speaker at conferences and business meetings. Connect with Sherrin at www.StrategicThinkers.org and www.Sherrin.com.

Barbara Niven

Shine Your Light

"Our deepest fear is not that we are inadequate. Our deepest fear is that we are powerful beyond measure."*

I'm sitting on a toilet in front of hundreds of people. On a stage in a high school auditorium, I share my story, I tell my truth. "We all have secrets," I say, looking out into an audience full of fresh, expectant faces. "I spent thirty years with my head hanging over a toilet, like this one, and no one ever knew. I was desperate to be perfect and I thought throwing up every day was my way to achieve perfection. It was my magic secret. My secret weapon. And my secret shame."

I go on to talk about chubby little me, the girl I still see when I look in the mirror. I always tried to make everyone happy, wearing big glasses and an even bigger smile. I pushed myself to be the good girl, the *perfect* girl. It meant that I often stuffed down my own emotions, ideas and aspirations. I never felt skinny enough, smart enough, or "perfect" enough, so I just tried harder. I would be devastated if I got less than A++ on my report cards. In third grade I wrote a novel and did so much extra credit that I got migraines, so they actually did an intervention to ban me from doing homework for the rest of the year. It crushed me. Over-achievers often develop eating disorders, and I was exhibiting all the classic warning signs even then.

From my perch on the toilet I talk about how, at age fifteen, I discovered a way to literally purge my feelings and "control" my weight. I describe my long battle for perfection as an actress in size-zero Hollywood, and the terrifying moment I woke up and accepted that I needed help.

> *"It is our light, not our darkness that most frightens us. We ask ourselves, Who am I to be brilliant, gorgeous, talented, fabulous? Actually, who are you not to be?"**

I stay late after each presentation, as I always do, and many people come up to talk to me about their daughters, their girlfriends, their students. And they ask for help for the adults in their life too, friends and family members who are suffering with eating disorders. Once again, I see that the statistics are very real: The largest growing demographic for eating disorders are women over forty.

> *The largest growing demographic for eating disorders are women over forty.*

Just as there are common triggers for young women (and to a lesser extent, young men), there are common triggers for aging women as well. Careers are in flux, nests empty, marriages go stale or breakup. Menopause hits, parents become ill or pass away and time speeds up so fast, you feel like you're running out of it. It's hard when you know you're never going to be as pretty as you once were, that it's all kind of going downhill. Yet the media feeds us images of what we're supposed to look like at forty, fifty, sixty and you believe you have to live up to that unrealistic ideal. And if you're already living a compromised life, trying to be "perfect" in other ways, these triggers can set you over the edge.

We all have secrets, and underneath these secrets is a fear so deep, it can take a lifetime to uncover it. As Marianne Williamson says so brilliantly in her iconic poem, it is the fear that we are "powerful beyond measure." We fear our own light, our own genius, our own destiny. We're afraid to be real, to be all that we are and all that God intended us to be, and so we hide the light within us... and this is how we become susceptible to destructive coping mechanisms.

How can you stand to hide your own light? How do you cope with the fear that underneath it all you are a shining star, especially if you've spent your whole life selling out? How are you able to continue to pretend that you are not designed for greatness when down deep, you know that you are? You eat. You purge. You shop. You gamble. You use. You avoid. You distract yourself with everything and anything that will help you forget the truth, that you are a "brilliant, gorgeous, talented, fabulous" woman.

"You are a child of God. Your playing small does not serve the world. There is nothing enlightened about shrinking so that other people won't feel insecure around you."

Some people would look at my life and assume that I've always "played big," when in fact I was holding myself back... just as I held my hair back as I vomited my feelings into the toilet day after day. Sure, I took the risk, packed up my young daughter and moved from Oregon to Los Angeles in pursuit of my dream. Yes, I made that dream come true, acting "as if" it was a reality until it absolutely *was*.

But I still lived with secrets. My age. My bulimia. My fear of never being good enough. I threw up because I couldn't talk about the real me, couldn't reveal that I was screaming inside to get out. And I was dying a little more every day.

I remember the day my sister called me out about my "big" secret. My sisters and I had flown home to Portland to help our mother pass away. Mom was an amazing woman, and losing her was devastating for our family. During the hospice process, I handled my stress the way I always did, by throwing it up into a toilet. It was so stressful I was doing it three or four times a day.

One day I came out of the bathroom to find my sister standing there, waiting for me. "I know what you did," she said. I was so angry with her for calling me out! "You have to get help," she said. Just to shut her up, I agreed, but I had no intention of getting help. Bulimia was my "magic secret," and I wasn't giving it up.

A couple of weeks after my mom passed away I received a phone call from my daughter's school. "Jessica fainted," the nurse said. I raced down there and discovered that she and her friends had been throwing up to fit into their cute little cheerleading uniforms. That was my worst fear come true. Like mother, like

> *Bulimia was my "magic secret," and I wasn't giving it up.*

daughter. It took two days for me to drum up the courage to do it, but I *did* make the call and ask for help.

That day, I found my voice. It would take years of therapy and practice and healing—for me and for Jessica—before I was able to actually use it consistently. But I found it. Later, I read the Marianne Williamson poem I'm quoting throughout this story, and I remembered: *there is a light in me!* In my search for "perfection" I had dimmed my own light to the point where I forgot it existed. I was always trying to be the perfect little girl, the perfect student, the perfect wife, and I never let my own voice come through. I assumed I had to be "perfect" in order to shine, when in truth all I needed to do was be honest and use my voice.

> *"We are all meant to shine, as children do. We were born to make manifest the glory of God that is within us. It's not just in some of us; it's in everyone."**

Only when you stop trying to be "perfect" and use your *real* voice can you truly excel. I've seen it time and time again with my clients, my colleagues and my friends. The real stars, the *superstars*, they have a heart-connection with audiences— and you can't have a heart-connection with *anyone* if you're not standing in your own truth. When I finally started using my voice and stopped trying to be Little Miss Perfect, everything got better: my acting, my career, my relationships. My whole world opened up, and suddenly I wasn't playing small anymore.

You have a mission and a message, and the world needs to hear it. But how can you change the world if you hold yourself back and play small? What are you waiting for? Your own unique, extraordinary star power is within you. All you need to do is dial it up. I know you've felt it before—moments when you're filled with passion, radiating with purpose, inspiring those around you. That is you playing big. That is you shining full out! What could you accomplish if you lived like that all the time? What if we all did?

"And as we let our own light shine, we unconsciously give other people permission to do the same. As we are liberated from our own fear, our presence automatically liberates others."*

Despite my decades of acting experience, I am scared every time I step onto the stage, confront that toilet and tell my truth. But I do it. I reveal my secret so that others will get the courage to speak up too. We must get rid of secrets that keep us sick, and use our stories to empower others.

So let's do this together. I'll make a pact with you: I promise to share my light and truth and power with you, and in turn you can share yours with someone else, and we'll keep paying it forward. Together we will start a blaze that can truly heal this planet, one beautiful light at a time!

Your life is a gift. You are here for a reason. Let this be the day. Start right now. Speak up. Be a FORCE. Shine your light. We are waiting.

*Excerpted from the poem by Marianne Williamson, from her book *Return to Love.*

Barbara Niven is one of Hollywood's busiest actresses, and has more than 2500 TV, film and commercial roles to her credit. You've seen her starring on Lifetime, Hallmark, NCIS, Cold Case *and* One Life To Live. *Barbara has also become Hollywood's top media coach. She created "Unleash Your Star Power!"™ to help others excel in videos, TV and radio interviews and public speaking. Clients include business owners, CEOs, speakers, authors and anyone who wants to make over their professional image. From her studio in Los Angeles, she offers custom video production services, one-on-one coaching and workshops. Her new book* 111 Star Power Tips – Insider Secrets From a Hollywood Pro *and the "Unleash Your Star Power!"™* Home Study Course *have just been released. She has appeared on national television talking about the pressure to be thin in Hollywood, and speaks to corporations and campuses about eating disorder prevention and recovery. Connect with Barbara at www.BarbaraNiven.com and www.UnleashYourStarPower.com.*

Mai Lieu

Intuition + Intention = Your Dream Fulfilled

This is it: Here I am, the spokesperson for my invention, live in front of millions worldwide on the Home Shopping Network. Orders come pouring in at red zone rates. Within thirteen minutes, I've sold out thousands of units! This is the dream some told me was impossible. The difference this time was that I had a great idea, *and* I let my intuition guide me straight to my dreams.

I'd been a successful, award-winning hairstylist for some years when a personal and professional growth seminar got me brainstorming about what I wanted *more of* from life. Work was stable, but I craved financial liberty and growth.

Once I started exploring, the universe brought me the idea: My clients were always cutting their own hair between salon visits, and without fail, I would have to fix it. I would invent a tool to help people easily cut their own hair at home, and sell it on TV—"Call and order now!" My intuition shouted, "This is *it!*"

When I told my colleagues that I had a great idea for an invention, something that would make millions, some of them laughed in my face and said, "Yeah, right, be realistic." I remember the hurt so clearly, but I turned that energy into a burning desire. I thought, *I'll show them!* Has anyone ever told you that you can't do something, and so influenced you into selling out your dreams? Because I was following my intuition, my inner voice, negativity didn't hold me back. I trusted the idea that miracles follow strong action guided by intuition. I trusted myself, and my vision.

I believe the universe brings us ideas all the time, and if we don't take action, that same idea will pass to others until finally someone does. I've had ideas for inventions since I was eight. Ten years after I dreamed them, I would see them in stores. I knew I had a gift. This time, instead of selling out, I sold out!

What is the gift that you are holding back from the world? I started with a prototype made from papier-mâché and chicken wire. How inspiring it was to watch my vision take tangible form! It was huge, nothing like it is now, but it worked. And as I tested

> *What is the gift that you are holding back from the world?*

it, changed it, brainstorming away, I'd wake up in the middle of the night humming with inspiration, full of possible solutions. I'd found my passion. And it manifested first in that little bestseller called the CreaClip.

It was a big risk, quitting my job and starting my own business. But I pushed through fears of not knowing how to bring my product to market and did it.

I had my fingers in everything from filing a patent to manufacturing and marketing. My determination paid off: things manifested like miracles, just by my asking. The moment I said, "I need a packaging designer," exactly the person I needed called me on the phone.

Fast-forward two years to the Home Shopping Network launch: total momentum. I often don't acknowledge myself how huge it was. For instance, I had the biggest fear of public speaking and no experience speaking in front of a small group, let alone millions. And I had to do it live on TV world-wide. That kind of fear makes your stomach turn and your hands shake. I remember being so clear that my goal was to sell out, no matter what. Talk about being outside your comfort zone!

Both my parents are entrepreneurs. When we came to Canada, we were poor and had nothing. But I watched my mom turn a two-thousand-dollar basement venture into a multimillion-dollar sportswear manufacturing business through trust, determination and persistence. In the early days, she managed to go out and get purchase orders for her clothing line without even being able to speak English. These values were instilled in me subconsciously as I saw her create results. I did not doubt that I could do it, too. Both Mom and Dad taught me exercises in positive thinking, too, that I use every day. The most important influence on your success is your own mind.

My biggest advice to you is to practice awareness. Then you can learn to tell the difference between the voice of your intuition, which will guide you to exactly where you need to be in every

> *When I committed to my dream 100% and set a clear intention, the whole universe conspired to help me, bringing me the solutions and people I needed and leading me to success.*

moment, and the voice of your conditioning, which keeps you locked up in fear. Making decisions based on fear can cause you to give up. When you learn to tune into your intuition alone, it will tell you your passion and purpose. And it gives you a sense of confidence and peace that will help you make the right decisions. When I committed to my dream 100% and set a clear intention, the whole universe conspired to help me, bringing me the solutions and people I needed and leading me to success.

Yes, it's hard work sometimes, pursuing a big dream! But there's no such thing as an obstacle. An obstacle is only an obstacle if you perceive it that way. Trusting that everything happens for a reason means I'm not discouraged by setbacks some might see as failures. When my first infomercial for the CreaClip didn't turn out the way I wanted, for instance, I felt strong doubt at first. *Maybe this was all a big mistake.* But when I trusted that everything happens for a purpose and realigned with my intention, I turned things around.

Then I filmed a home video of a friend cutting her hair with the CreaClip and posted the video on YouTube. Within months, my videos had been viewed nearly one million times. Since then my sales have gone up over 5000% and continue to grow each month. All from free marketing! What had *seemed* like an obstacle was actually a gift. Plan A not working forced me to find the Plan B that turned into a triumph. I know now that when I have a struggle, eventually I'll look back and say, "See? It was perfect just as it was."

Each day brings more to be grateful for. I have distribution in Japan, and am talking with potential partners in the United Kingdom and Israel. And because my intuition is definitely my

> *I know now that when I have a struggle, eventually I'll look back and say, "See? It was perfect just as it was."*

creative voice, I keep inventing new products, including a line of lingerie for feet, "RisQue by Mai Lieu," recently spotted on many celebrities at Hollywood's sneak-peek Oscar events.

After consulting with fellow inventors, I find their greatest fear is that they do not know how to do everything, and that causes them to give up easily.

I'm here to tell you, you don't need to know how to do everything. When I started, I was a hairstylist with no experience in product development. All you have to do is figure out what you want and listen to your intuition; set your intention by developing a clear vision; commit and stay positive. After that, everything falls into place.

Not to say you just sit on your couch and wait, at that point. Once your intuition starts to speak, you need to act. When you are living your passion, it won't feel like work, because whatever it is, you'll love doing it. No one will have to force you out of bed in the morning if you're trusting in yourself and your dreams. Your intention is a grounding, energizing force that makes anything possible—even the so-called "impossible."

What's your "impossible" dream? I challenge you to listen to your intuition, set your intention and go for it!

Mai Lieu is an inventor and entrepreneur and president, CEO and founder of Innov8 LLC, dba CreaProducts, a product development and consulting firm, that empowers and inspires through its creative products. During fifteen years in the beauty industry, Mai won seven first-place international hairdressing awards. She has worked and trained in the United States, Canada, China and Europe. In 2008, Mai was recognized in Cambridge Who's Who *as one of the top four businesswomen (out of half a million). She was also nominated and a finalist for the Stevie Award's "Best New Product of the Year" in both 2009 and 2010 for the CreaClip, an ingenious hair trimming guide which sold out on the Home Shopping Network. Her success story was featured in the bestselling book* The Law of Business Attraction, *in many periodicals and on numerous TV and radio stations. Connect with Mai at www.CreaClip.com.*

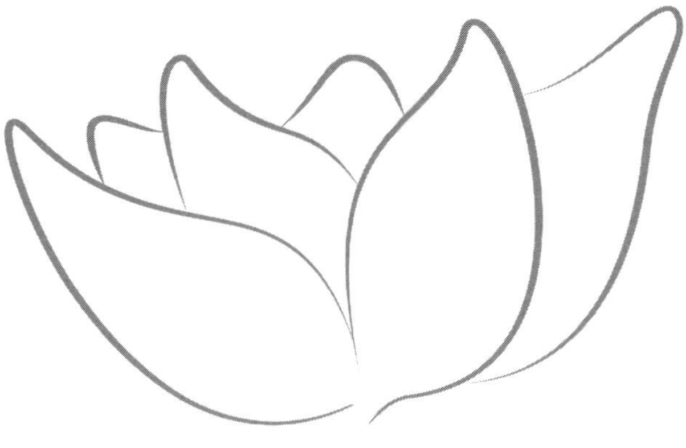

Dr. Linda Brodsky

Only She Who Attempts the Absurd Will Achieve the Impossible

It was December 26, 2007. I held a $740,000 check in my hand. After fighting for gender equity for nearly eight years, I had recently settled my case with the university. I still had two lawsuits to conclude with the Children's Hospital of Buffalo, in New York. This money would be just enough to cover my legal fees. Still, I felt a deep sense of satisfaction. I had survived, and I was hopeful. I had stood up to two large and powerful organizations so I could change the world for all women who might experience gender discrimination.

Everyone will take notice! They will stand up and cheer, I thought. But they didn't. *Others will be inspired by what I did.* But they weren't. *I know my life will change for the better.* But it didn't.

As the weeks and months passed, my life did change, but not as I had expected. I was banned from any contact with students and residents. I was cast out from the medical academic world in Buffalo. I was demeaned and marginalized and ignored. I no longer felt hopeful. Instead I felt diminished and very alone. What had I really gained and for whom?

When I became a surgeon—something very difficult for a woman thirty years ago—I knew I would rise to the top of my profession. I wanted to reach beyond helping only my own patients. I devoted time to the difficult path of academic medicine, conducting research and teaching at a medical center. But I was met with the shocking reality that strong, assertive, successful women were not welcome in medical academia.

I knew in medical school that I had to become a surgeon. I loved the fast pace, the almost immediate gratification and the intense focus in the moment of saving a life.

After four years of grueling training in otolaryngology in New York, I went to the Children's Hospital of Buffalo for further training. I became a "super specialist," a pediatric otolaryngologist—an ear, nose and throat surgeon for kids. Fixing little airways so babies

> *I no longer felt hopeful. Instead I felt diminished and very alone. What had I really gained and for whom?*

could breathe, mastering delicate, microscopic ear surgeries so children could hear and removing dangerous neck tumors so families could see their children grow up healthy—this was my destiny.

In 1984, I accepted a position in academic medicine at the University at Buffalo. I was the only woman surgeon on staff at the hospital, and the only full-time female faculty member in any surgical department at the university.

The twelve-year climb to the top of my field was difficult and often lonely. I was a very busy surgeon. And I also wrote dozens of articles, lectured on four continents and received many awards and research grants. I mentored dozens of medical students and resident trainees and assumed many leadership positions. I was chosen to spearhead and then lead the Center for Pediatric Quality, a hospital-wide physician-driven effort to improve quality. I had reached the highest rank of tenured full Professor of Otolaryngology and Pediatrics and was one of only about twelve women in the United States in 1996 to reach this prestigious professorial rank in my field. My colleagues in Buffalo fondly crowned me the "Queen of ENT."

Was there anything I couldn't do? Nothing that I could ever imagine, certainly not then. What was next?

In 1997, two major leadership roles became available—university chair and hospital department head. I knew I was up for each task, and had demonstrated the necessary leadership skills. Yet despite my qualifications, which only one year before resulted in my being offered a chair position at another institution, I was passed over. A male with neither academic credentials nor an international reputation was appointed as interim chair. I was crushed.

I resolved to work harder and to apply for the permanent chair. But what I discovered next was even more shocking. I learned that the university was compensating at twice my salary a recently hired male ENT faculty member with lower rank, no seniority and fewer responsibilities!

> *I was faced with an unsettling truth:*
> *the system I believed in and worked hard*
> *to be a part of was controlled by an old boys*
> *club that placed the status quo above excel-*
> *lence, achievement and creativity.*

I soon discovered that my male surgical colleagues at the hospital were being paid as much as five times my salary for their hospital administrative work and teaching. None of them even came close to my experience. I had been director of one of the busiest and most successful clinical services for more than a decade. It had never occurred to me that at the turn of the twenty-first century, I might be a victim of gender discrimination! But there it was, smacking me right in the face. The deeper I looked, the more troubled I became.

I was faced with an unsettling truth: the system I believed in and worked hard to be a part of was controlled by an old boys club that placed the status quo above excellence, achievement and creativity. This realization was one harsh awakening. Confused, angry and very hurt, I pressed on, focusing on working within the system to get what was equitable. My only reward was escalating harassment and retaliation for raising the issue. As terrible as it feels to think that you've been treated unfairly, it feels even worse to think that the perpetrators might get away with it.

Almost three years later, I filed seven complaints with the Equal Employment Opportunity Commission. Eighteen months after that, I received my "right to sue" letters. I then filed my first claim in federal court in 2001. For the next six years, I was on a crusade. I spent all of my political capital and all of the gains I had

> *One of my favorite passages from the Old Testament (and my son's Bar Mitzvah portion) is, "Justice, justice shall thou pursue" (Deuteronomy 16:20).*

made throughout my entire career up to that point to set it right. I knew that, no matter what I would ultimately "win," I would never again be offered a chair anywhere. I would never again be welcome in mainstream leadership in medicine. I had so much to lose. And I had no choice.

But I do not do the "victim" thing well. After the fog of disappointment cleared, I realized my crusade had not come to an end. My memoirs were on my mind, but it was too early, too painful and the struggle was not yet over. I started to receive calls from many other women who had heard about my fight. They needed help.

I found renewed hope and a new mission: women physicians had to be fully and fairly integrated into the healthcare system. And I decided that I would help to expedite what I knew was inevitable.

Fifty percent of medical school graduates and thirty percent of physicians are women. Our society cannot afford to allow the skills of even one highly-trained doctor go to waste. Our current social awareness of the need for women to be treated equitably and become a valued part of the physician workforce will inevitably drive the workplace of tomorrow. It is time that the medical workplace retooled to face this inevitability.

Expediting the Inevitable is an organization devoted to tapping into the workforce of women physicians. We bring individuals, organizations, institutions and others together to collaborate on the best way each element can function for the common goal of better health and better medical care. A more open and flexible medical workplace environment enlarges our talent pool. The workplace for women physicians must and will foster the full integration, creativity and success we seek.

One of my favorite passages from the Old Testament (and my son's Bar Mitzvah portion) is, "Justice, justice shall thou pursue" (Deuteronomy 16:20). I have always bristled at unfair situations. Pursuing justice, improving quality, and making the world a better place is part of my heritage, part of my life. My journey started as a personal quest. I faced many trials and took many detours. But I stuck with it, no matter how difficult, because I believe that one voice can, did and will make a difference.

I learned that it is not easy to change the world. But I had to fight. Being an impassioned crusader is not something I fell into; it's who I have been from the beginning and will be until the end of my life. Not everyone need choose such a difficult battle. But every one of us can change the world in some way, large or small. First, look in the mirror and ask, "Do I have the courage of my convictions? Can I follow my heart?" If you do, then don't turn away. Don't settle. The path may not be easy. Go forward. You can make a difference. Together we can make a difference.

Not long ago a family came to my office. They had seen three other doctors, but the child was still sick. Her mother pleadingly told me, "I came to you because I hear you're a miracle worker."

I laughed somewhat nervously while I assured her I was not.

She replied, "Well, I heard you never give up." I knew what she said was true. I was proud to have that reputation.

Sometimes never giving up IS the miracle. If you believe in something so strongly that you cannot let it go, let it be *your* crusade. Take the risk. The win might be small, or it can be huge—even when you are not sure you have won at all. So never, never, never give up, especially on your dreams. Believe that *you* can attempt the absurd, and indeed, achieve the impossible.

Dr. Linda Brodsky is an award-winning pediatric otolaryngologist, surgeon, patient advocate and crusader for gender equity in medicine. She has been named a "Best Doctor in America" since 1992. She holds an AB from Bryn Mawr College and received her medical education at the Women's Medical College of Pennsylvania. Her residency training in otolaryngology was at the Albert Einstein College of Medicine/ Montefiore Hospital and Medical Center in Bronx, New York, followed by a fellowship in pediatric otolaryngology at the Children's Hospital of Buffalo.

Linda's decades-long career at the Women and Children's Hospital of Buffalo and the University at Buffalo included numerous appointments and professorships. She was Director of Pediatric Otolaryngology and Communication Disorders and a tenured full Professor of Otolaryngology and Pediatrics. Linda was the founder and Director of the Center of Pediatric Quality at the Women and Children's Hospital of Buffalo. Connect with Linda at www.LindaBrodskyMD. com and www.ExpeditingtheInevitable.com.

Suzane Piela, RN

Sacred Passage

The phone rings to my mother's voice crying on the other end. "Susie, your father has cancer." Several months pass, another phone call with Mom crying. "Susie, I have cancer." Shortly thereafter, my father died. Then a third poignant phone call from Mom. Her chemotherapy no longer working, she asks if I can come and be with her for a couple of weeks. "I want your spirituality. I saw how you were with your father's dying and I want what you have."

Sensing she was asking for more than a short time, I went into prayer. That night my answer came in a dream. My father arrived to pick me up in an old flatbed truck from my childhood. I'm on the back and we are flying above the treetops, the wind gently blowing in my face. The scene changes and I'm in my parents' bedroom standing in the corner watching them talk to each other. It feels very peaceful. Then my father leaves and I'm alone with Mom. The dream ends. The next day I gave notice at my job. Two weeks later my life as I knew it in Los Angeles ended.

Normally I'm not a woman who makes life-altering decisions quickly. And answers to my prayers don't normally happen through a vivid dream. But then my parents' illnesses within months of each other weren't normal times. When my mother reached out for help, which she rarely did for fear of being a burden on her children, it was clear my life was being guided in a different direction. My friends called my decision courageous. I didn't see it that way. It was simply a choice-less choice leading me back to the woman who gave me birth.

My mother and sister met me at the small rural airport in Wisconsin on a warm summer afternoon. I felt an unsettledness as I hugged Mom, a feeling of being unanchored from the familiarity of my old life. I was surprised by how healthy she looked in spite of the wig hiding her bald head.

She asked me how long I could stay.

I said, "As long as you need me, Mom." I sensed her relief at my response.

Then, two hours later, I was back in the upstairs bedroom I had shared with my two sisters growing up. A crucifix still hung in the same place on the wall, the same wrought-iron double bed stood by the same old chest of drawers, the same baseboard vent would allow limited heat from the old furnace in the basement. Outside the only window in the small room, the lilac tree was still firmly rooted in the same place. It seemed nothing—and everything— had changed. This wasn't going back to visit my parents for a week and then returning to the security of my own life. This now was my life.

Nine months earlier they had been the healthy backbone of our family structure, Mom the glue that held us together. All that was shattered and I was alone with Mom, who was grieving the loss of her husband of almost fifty years, the life they built together and the loss of her health. She needed me, and in the days ahead I found myself needing what we would share together.

Here were two seemingly opposite women with the unique qualities, quirks and frailties that had defined our roles. One chose tradition as a farm wife, raising seven children; the other chose to have no children and to discover herself outside of a marriage. *Who were we separate from our roles and what gifts were we imparting to each other?* I hungered to know the woman Mom was, apart from being my mother.

When I returned to care for her, she had only one request of me—hold the hope that she would be cured of her cancer. I agreed, not realizing what a challenge that would become as her health declined. As she had been a rock for me, sometimes late at night after she was tucked safely in bed I would lie upstairs crying and praying for the strength to be her rock in the vulnerability of her dying. Although I had cared for dying patients, having it be my loved one was a whole different picture. I felt alone, realizing I didn't know how to 'be' on a day-to-day basis with her. In our family we were always doers—some chore always needing to be done—the safety net from emotional openness and vulnerability with each other.

> *I learned to trust being in the moment of each day and to look for the pearls in the oyster.*

There was no escaping that emotional landscape, my fears, doubts, old patterns, beliefs, and my ability to care for her— everything was naked in front of me. I would be reminded of the mystical words of a New Year's ceremony the year before when I sat on a mountaintop praying for the blending of my life's purpose with my vocation. "Blessings, sweet child of the Light. You are asked to take on the challenges presented before you, if you so choose. You have the capacity and will reap great rewards." So I learned to trust being in the moment of each day and to look for the pearls in the oyster.

We eventually found a groove, like a newly married couple learning each other's nuances. We would spend hours talking about anything and everything, wherever our conversations would take us.

There became a womb-like quality being with her. My soul became re-rooted with nature, my body was again in the rhythm and cycle of changing seasons. As they shed their coats, so did I shed the emotional walls.

A deepening intimacy transpired in our relationship. I felt like she had become an umbilical cord to a rebirth and re-discovery of myself and I was an umbilical cord birthing her through the sacred journey of her dying. I would savor her ways of being: how she read her prayer book each morning, how she put ketchup on her breakfast eggs, the way she would wring her hands in worry, the laughter of her voice.

For the last few days of her life, the living room became her respite and the couch her security of hibernation. Using a TV tray, I arranged a geranium flower from her garden, her rosary, the crucifix from her bedroom and candles to create an altar and placed it at the head of the couch. Mom's favorite music played softly in the background.

> *Our roles had reversed—*
> *through our journey together the daughter*
> *had become the parent, cradling her essence*
> *just as she did when I was a baby.*

The day of her passing, a huge thunderstorm rippled through the sky and I whispered to Mom that God was cleaning the heavens for her. Afterward, the sun shone through our big picture window projecting a glow around her face. Birds started singing and hummingbirds sipped at the feeder she loved watching when she became too weak for anything else. Sometime during the evening, my sister and brother, who live a few miles from the homestead, stopped by to share happier memories of Mom. Others had called throughout the day to she how she was doing.

Knowing she would pass that night, I asked my brother and sister if they wanted to stay. They declined and again I was alone with Mom, watching the shallow, interspersed breaths of her remaining minutes. Our roles had reversed—through our journey together the daughter had become the parent, cradling her essence just as she did when I was a baby. It seemed fitting. I was giving back to the life that gave me life. My heart filled with love as I sat on the floor next to her holding her hand. Then she gently and quietly took her last breath.

With tears rolling down my face, I had a strong desire to bathe her. As I filled a basin of warm water and gathered her red robe, I felt drawn into an ancient time and another mystical experience. As if outside my body, I watched my hand wrapped around a washcloth, delicately washing her skin in a circular fashion, much the way she did with my younger brothers when they were babies. There was a strong knowing and familiarity to what I was doing. As she had asked, I plucked the hairs on her chin of which she had been self-conscious. When her body was nestled in her

> *Death is not an ending but rather the continuation of relationships in a different form.*

robe, I kissed the palms of both hands and folded them on her lap. Then from some place deep inside, a voice clearly and distinctly said, "It is done." The energy of the trance ended and I put my head on her lap and wept.

Several hours later when the mortuary attendants arrived, they commented on how incredibly peaceful it was in the house. "How wonderful for your mom to have died in this energy. Of all the people we have served throughout the years, this is the first time we have experienced this kind of peacefulness." With the sound of their vehicle tires on the gravel driveway in the early morning hours, the farmhouse was silent with all the memories its walls held. Lying upstairs, grateful for the year shared with Mom, I heard footsteps, first in the living room and then in the kitchen. They lasted a few minutes and then disappeared. I sensed my father had come to escort her to the other side and a new life together.

Death is not an ending but rather the continuation of relationships in a different form. Love is what feeds and expands our souls. Love is the true measure of our capacity as human beings, which connects us spiritually to everyone and all life. While birth is the miracle of life, death is the celebration of our essence that remains forever fragrant in the inner landscape of our hearts. This is ancient wisdom we have lost, an ancient wisdom that is our spiritual birthright in the beauty and grace of our sacred passage with life and death.

Suzane Piela, RN, is an inspirational speaker, author and visionary for global change. A graduate of the University of Wisconsin, she holds a BS in nursing and attended graduate school at Antioch University in Seattle. Suzane's desire to inspire conscious transformation led her to blend her nursing background with experiences in marketing and media promotions. An Executive Producer of Beyond the Line, *a television talk show exploring progressive thought on topics such as spirituality, near-death experience, water birthing and alternative medicine, she also served as co-producer for a video,* Awakenings: Times of Change & Promise.*

Suzane is a certified hypnotherapist, trained in healing energies, and a hospice nurse. For the past fifteen years she has centered her focus on the field of death and dying. Her mission is to transform the face of death into a sacred journey of rebirth. She is the published author of You Are So Beautiful Without Your Hair: A Daughter's Journey with the Death of Her Parents. *She is currently completing her second book on a step-by-step approach for sacred dying. Connect with Suzane at www.SuzanePiela.com.*

Rosemary Bredeson

The Leap: From Confusion to Clarity

The Space Telescope Science Institute was a zoo, its conference room crowded with hundreds of guests from around the world. The front driveway of the building was filled with news satellite trucks and press corps members speaking a cacophony of different languages into microphones of every size and shape. Three hundred and thirty nautical miles above the earth, a telescope the size of a school bus—our telescope, the Hubble Space Telescope— was poised to capture historic images of Comet Schumacher-Levy 9, which was expected to pass very near—or make contact with— the planet Jupiter.

As the head of the Hubble Telescope's Office of Public Outreach, I had organized a massive press conference to coincide with Hubble's transmissions of this event. None of us on staff knew what we'd see. The assembled crowd eagerly awaited Hubble's images of the comet's impact on Jupiter, while downstairs in the Operations Center, scientists, analysts, managers, publicists, computer wizards and interns with their eyes all directed through Hubble's own wondered if the telescope would even *pick up* an image of the event.

I'd started out in management, but moved to creating Hubble's Office of Public Outreach, and was responsible for bringing Hubble from space to Maryland to the world through press, education and distribution of imagery. All of this had felt pretty glamorous to me, I must admit.

The more spiritual work I did, however, the more I wondered why, exactly, I was there. It was exciting and important, a great boon to humanity, but I felt called to help at a different level of human consciousness. My intuition told me that Hubble was giving me a clue about my life's true path.

A great burst of excitement exploded in the Operations Center; not only was Hubble picking up images of Schumacher-Levy, it had just captured the comet bursting apart and making contact with Jupiter in a series of dramatic bangs that looked like dark spots appearing on the bright surface of the planet. Like First Light, when the first images from Hubble appeared years before, it was a champagne moment.

The crowd upstairs was still waiting to see these images. The press was waiting for an announcement. Something very exciting was happening, but it didn't feel real to me at all. Suddenly, I felt

> *My intuition told me that Hubble was giving me a clue about my life's true path.*

the urge to go outside. I walked out past the crowds and the movie-set-like collection of reporters and news trucks into an open space, where I stood staring up into the sky. I wanted to make my own connection, without anything between me and Jupiter. I wanted a direct experience of what was happening, rather than an artificial construct of pictures in a computer.

As I looked up at Jupiter in the night sky, I thought, *There's something more than this job. There's something bigger happening, and I need to be a part of it.* After twelve great years with Hubble, I knew that my work there was done. I needed to move into work that was fulfilling and rewarding in a very real sense. And I knew that my clarity was going to come directly from looking inward.

When I left my successful, glamorous career for one much less easy to define, I followed my gut and made a true leap of faith. I had already been studying tools like meditation, NLP and Reiki, tools that were helping me in my own life, but I wasn't sure what my calling was until that moment outside, looking up into the sky. But there comes a point in every transformation where it starts to be more uncomfortable to stay with the familiar than it does to make that leap.

Hubble had given me the clue I needed: I had been called to become a kind of Hubble Telescope for other people. When I listened to my intuition, I let it guide me to my work as an intuitive coach, a spiritual counselor, a mystic and a muse.

A quantum leap for humanity happened when Galileo first invented the telescope. But Galileo's vision was distorted by the Earth's atmosphere. It wasn't until we could see with the clarity of

Intuition does for the transformation of our lives what the Hubble does for humanity.

the Hubble—from beyond the atmosphere—that the revelations of the Universe could unfold before us.

This was another huge quantum leap for humanity. It didn't just mean we could see galaxies, stars, nebulae and planets in places that had once looked like blank, black spots; it meant we could see far, far out in time, measuring light beams that had begun traveling billions of years earlier. With this leap, we could now discuss the nature and age of the universe in ways we could not before seeing beyond the veil of the atmosphere.

Intuition does for the transformation of our lives what the Hubble does for humanity. Everybody has a moment when they need clarity and confidence. The question at that moment is, "How do I achieve this?"

The answer lies within you. Go inside. Trust what you find there. Trust that your intuition knows what you need and will show you the way. If you encounter blocks, get help in clearing them. Looking outside yourself for answers leads you away from your own empowerment, and this can keep you confused by what others tell you to do. Your clarity and confidence come from inside, from connecting your head, your heart and your gut.

Many of us know we have this inner voice, but we don't learn to trust it until we practice. Sometimes, we need a guide to show us how to do this. We spend a lot of time praying or talking to Spirit, but we forget to pause and listen for answers. We don't trust that intuition is how the answers come to us. But we humans do have this ability, this access to information and guidance. If we'd just go inside, stop talking and start listening, we would be able to hear what the guidance is trying to tell us.

We don't get how powerful our intuition is. It's part of the vernacular, we hear the word every day, but do we really think about what it means?

Our conscious minds can only handle seven, plus or minus two, chunks of information at any given time. Our unconscious minds are receiving *2.6 million* bits of information every second and storing that away in the database. Which would you rather work with? I'm going with the one that has the most information, which is the unconscious mind. Your intuition is how you access this database. Would you rather look at the cosmos from your front porch, or through the Hubble?

Once you trust that you can open up and access all this information that's been clouded by the atmosphere of your life, your limiting beliefs and other people's beliefs and thoughts, everything is available to you.

Intuition is essential for transformation because it is the message from the higher self to us to get our attention, to get us to focus on our life's purpose. If we ignore the avenues this information travels, we keep ourselves from growing. We keep ourselves from evolving. The images from Hubble come to us, and they're glorious to look at, but a whole team investigates the images for meaning. This is what we have to do to engage with the information we're receiving from our intuition. What's the message?

Women have this wonderful thing history has called "women's intuition." When we moved into the workplace, we thought we had to deny that part of ourselves to become powerful in business. By not trusting what we had always trusted while we cared for our children, prepared food and did all of those traditionally "womanly" things, we have tended not to trust and have confidence in ourselves in the workplace. But it is time to leverage our intuition in every aspect of our lives. Don't bifurcate, don't put your intuition in a corner just because you're a woman in the workplace—use it to your advantage.

To practice trusting your gut, you've really got to take that leap and commit to yourself. Take back your power and recognize that no one else can lead you to your life's purpose. Your field of

> *Basically, hit the pause button and you can listen to the voice of your inner guidance.*

possibility is endlessly vast. If you feel stuck, you may be so focused on a challenge that you forget your intuition has the solution. Step out of this cloud of confusion by tapping into your inner wisdom.

Try meditation. It doesn't have to be anything formal; one breath can slow you into the place where you can hear your intuition. Basically, hit the pause button and you can listen to the voice of your inner guidance.

When you get to the next fork in the road, the first step you're going to take is to pause, breathe and ask your inner guide, "Which one, which path has more light on it? Show me that one." What follows from that is clarity about the next step. You start to get a clear picture of where you need to go. You start to get a clear picture of what's holding you back.

You need that clarity before you can move forward. It's like adjusting the lenses on a telescope to discover the vast beauty of your own universe and the possibilities before you. Because it is not being impeded, your unconscious mind will now begin to work toward your goals.

You start walking forward with consciousness, clarity and confidence. You become aware. You notice. You ask the questions that help you continue to grow and expand on your journey and to touch others in a positive way. That's what being a transformational woman is all about—stepping into your own transformation and reaching out to help others realize theirs.

Rosemary Bredeson, BA, CMH, is an intuitive empowerment coach and medium who has worked with individuals and groups to advance their personal, business and spiritual development for more than twenty years. Using her entrepreneurial and business coaching experience, Rosemary empowers her clients to connect with their inner wisdom, including the unconscious mind and intuition, for guidance, clarity and confidence. Rosemary is also a multi-dimensional communications expert. This allows her to share wisdom from higher realms.

Rosemary uses many healing and development technologies and holds certifications as a Master Hypnotherapist (CMH), Trainer of Hypnotherapy, Master Practitioner of HNLP, Reiki Master and Pastoral Counselor. She also holds a BA in mathematics, and worked with NASA on the Hubble Space Telescope project for twelve years. Rosemary is the founder and CEO of A New Alliance for Change LLC, a personal development center in Colorado. She is the author of This Year: Live Your Richest Life *and* 50 Questions for The Other Side. *Connect with Rosemary at www.TheScientificMystic.com.*

Joy Leach

The Power of Choice

Sitting next to my husband Rich on the lawn at Boston College, waiting for our son Ian to walk across the stage and accept his diploma, I looked out at the sea of proud parents and wondered what choices brought them to this moment. What did they do absolutely right? What compromises did they make? What did they give up that they wished they hadn't?

I was pretty sure most of them made different choices than we had, and not just because we were underdressed for this East Coast ceremony in our California casual attire. As primary provider for my family for nearly three decades, I knew that I was probably in the minority among the other mothers present that day.

Years ago, if you would have asked me why—why I chose this path, why I endured the long workdays, the frequent business trips and feeling so torn between my career and my kids I feared I would break in two—more often than not I would have said, "Because I want to give our kids a stellar education."

But that was before I started writing a book. I'd long planned to write a book to help couples like us stay in love and lead satisfying lives, and in the January preceding Ian's graduation I re-committed to the project.

Writing *She Earns More* forced me to dig deeper, to take an honest look at, well, everything.

With the last tuition payment sent and Ian on his way, I had the option to ease up, but no plans to do so. I still said "yes" to my clients, packed my go-to black business separates in my carry-on and went to work. *What's driving you now, Joy?* I wondered. Hadn't I looked forward to this time, to the freedom to pursue other interests and earn less money? Were my aspirations fueled by something deeper and more ingrained than the immediate need of providing a certain lifestyle for my family?

Looking for answers, I came back to my earliest choices. My mother, who worked in the home and at our family's Italian restaurant in Elmira, New York, never earned a paycheck. Once a week my father, the sole owner of the restaurant, would give my

> *I respected my mother for making it work—but every time I watched my father pull seven dollars from a wad of cash in his pocket, the days' earnings, I could see that she was powerless.*

mother seven one-dollar bills. From this allowance she would take care of me, my four older siblings, our home, and—in the rare event any money was left over—herself.

My mother was very resourceful—she made a lot of magic happen for very little money. I still remember the gorgeous, sea-green appliquéd silk organza dress she had made for me for my eighth grade graduation. I never knew the deal she struck with the Italian immigrant who made the dress, or how, despite not having her own car, she made it to watch me cheer at elementary school games. But I did know how she managed to fund the dance classes I took from the time I was five until I was a senior in high school: She "stole" the money from my father's pocket.

He must have known she was sneaking more than her allotted seven dollars so I could take the classes I loved. He *must* have known, because every once in a while, an argument would erupt. And yet the lessons continued. That meant that each time my dance teacher requested payment, my mother had to sneak money from her own husband in her own home. I respected my mother for making it work—but every time I watched my father pull seven dollars from a wad of cash in his pocket, the days' earnings, I could see that she was powerless.

I learned very early that I could either succumb to feeling oppressed by a situation, or I could fight it. So from the time I was a young girl, I vowed I would never let anybody determine what

> For years—decades, even—
> I thought Rich and I had made a
> mutual decision about our roles.

I could or could not do or have. I made an invisible agreement with myself: *No one will hold you back. You will get what you want. No matter what, you will never be dependent on someone else for money.*

Though I later learned that my powerful, rebellious energy has some inherent costs, it was this invisible agreement which propelled me into action. When I took my first job as a waitress at age fourteen, when I entered my first college class, when I earned my degree, when I accepted my first job as a social worker, when I defied convention and bought my own duplex as a single woman in my twenties, this invisible agreement gave me the inspiration and the will to push on.

After Rich and I married and moved to Boulder, Colorado, I taught an assertiveness training class for women at night. Even then, I was trying to create a different outcome for my mother by teaching other women how to be more assertive, more powerful. One night a man sat in on the class, and after I finished, he asked, "Would you be willing to take this training on the road?" In an instant, I went from making five bucks an hour to earning seven-hundred-fifty dollars a day.

It was the beginning of my career as a corporate trainer—and my role as the main breadwinner.

For years—decades, even—I thought Rich and I had made a mutual decision about our roles. We had, but that wasn't the whole story.

After looking back at my formative experiences, I now understand that the invisible agreement I made with myself as a child compelled me to say *yes* to all of it. *Yes* to the lifestyle my career could provide. *Yes* to the fun of succeeding in business. *Yes* to the freedom, and the adventure. *Yes* to the pressures of providing

> *When a decision is made early in life, it can actually co-opt choice later in life.*

a high level of income for my family. *Yes* to hearing my daughter Maris' cry from a hotel room when I took her on the road with me as an infant. *Yes* to longing to see my husband and my kids, and *yes* to feeling guilty about missing out on so much of the day-to-day.

There were definite upsides, but the downside of living according to my earliest choices was never really asking myself, *What do I truly value here?* Was it my value to leave my kid at six weeks to go back to work? I know I didn't want to leave Ian, but I was afraid that if I stayed home for six months, I wouldn't be able to "get back on the horse." Was it my value to give up on my doctorate? Again, I chose not to risk taking time off from my business to do what I wanted to do.

Could we have lived on Rich's income? Absolutely. But I just couldn't let myself depend on Rich for money. I couldn't give up my autonomy, or my power. So I unconsciously set up scenarios in which I had to earn, earn, earn. A nicer house in a better neighborhood. Private school for the kids. No rainy-day fund in place so I could slow down or take a break.

If I could do it over again, I might choose to say, "I'm going to earn less and manage my fear of depending on someone else, or manage my fear of re-entering the workplace after a break." I would look from the inside out as I made the most important choices in my life.

When a decision is made early in life, it can actually co-opt choice later in life. I let my early invisible agreement define who I was and determine what I would and would not do. Most of the time, it afforded us an amazing, exciting, gratifying life. But sometimes, it compelled me to push on even when it wasn't the best decision for me or for my family. In my determination to be independent, I actually ended up limiting my choices.

These "invisible agreements," whether we make them with ourselves, with our partners, or with others, shape our relationships. For example, Rich and I made an early invisible agreement about my role as provider. When I started making two, sometimes three, times as much as Rich could earn on his best, most productive day, we silently agreed that I would stay in the provider role indefinitely. Here again I unconsciously limited my choices by entering into a "binding" agreement with myself, and with Rich.

I've made a new agreement with myself—to make conscious choices, rather than just act out of an early script. Early agreements and ingrained patterns can leave us as constrained as women were before the feminist movement, when their only choice was to become teachers, secretaries or nuns—or not work outside of the home at all. Even the expectation to get an MBA and earn six figures can be confining if it does not fulfill you or limits your choices.

How can we forge ahead with full awareness, creating authentic lives of joy and fulfillment? As our roles continue to shift, I hope that all women—especially those who are in dual-income marriages, or who earn more than their partners—look beyond labels to find their true value and deepest desires. Be honest with yourself. Make agreements and decisions consciously, cooperatively; leave room for the "you" that is yet to come. This is my hope for my daughter. This is my hope for myself. This is my hope for *you*.

Joy Leach has devoted her life to helping people unravel the challenges they face in today's workplace and home lives. Over the course of her twenty-five-year career as an organizational consultant, trainer, executive coach and author, Joy has talked with more than forty-thousand women and men about glass ceiling and gender issues, diversity and work/life balance. As President and co-founder of Professional Resources Initiatives (www.GlobalPRI.com), Joy has worked with hundreds of organizations, including Pfizer, Mattel, PWC and MasterCard. An acclaimed public speaker, Joy is currently writing her third book, She Earns More: Creating a Joyous Life from Bank to Bedroom. *Connect with Joy at www.SheEarnsMore.com.*

Clare Dreyer

Evolving Out of the Blue

*P*eople *really live here?* I thought, as I surveyed the view of the stunning Sierra Nevada mountains. As far as I could see, I was surrounded by majestic snow-capped peaks, and the sparkling, crystalline waters of a deep mountain lake. *Yes, silly,* was my next thought, people really do live here—*and so do you.*

When I moved to beautiful Lake Tahoe from Florida a few weeks earlier to start my new life, I was forty-eight years old and newly single (again). It was a move and a life change that I had not expected or anticipated, and for which I was completely unprepared. Shortly after I started my new job, one of my colleagues invited me to a cocktail party. As I chatted with one of the local women there, she asked me, "So what do you do, Clare?"

"Do?" I replied. "Well, for years I had my own consulting business, which—"

"No, no," she laughed, "I mean, what do you *do?* Do you hike, mountain bike, ski? What?"

I was dumbfounded. I had always defined myself by my roles— wife, mother, business owner. What did I *do?* I realized in that moment, much to my dismay, that I didn't DO anything. There wasn't much I could say. In Florida, people don't hike; the alligators, swamps and mosquitoes kind of put the kibosh on that. But her question pointed to something deeper. These people didn't care how much money I made, whom I knew, or what I did for a living. Instead, they wanted to know *who* I was. What did I *enjoy* doing? In that moment, I vowed that the next time someone asked me, I'd have an answer.

Change happens. It can be sparked by a person, an event, or a flash of insight. For me, the catalyst for change was a divorce, followed by new surroundings and a career change. The place was Lake Tahoe, a clear, deep blue jewel of a lake that straddles California and Nevada and is ringed by soaring mountains, majestic forests and alpine meadows. Tahoe has always represented the spirit of freedom to me—the freedom to explore, to change and to grow. Now, in this magnificent place, I could do all of that for myself.

> *I was dumbfounded. I had always defined myself by my roles—wife, mother, business owner. What did I do? I realized in that moment, much to my dismay, that I didn't DO anything.*

My second marriage ended for all of the right reasons, and the divorce was my first bold move. My next daring step was moving to Tahoe, where I only knew two people. I then started a brand new career. The vow that I'd *do* something set off a chain reaction of many dynamic and positive changes in my life.

I had a bike. It was a fancy mountain bike. Having a bike like that in Florida never seemed quite right, but somehow it made sense when I bought it. I have always loved riding my bike; it has long been my avenue for escape. Growing up in Daytona Beach, I used to ride for hours up and down the beach, sometimes even arriving in time to catch the sunrise before I headed to school. As a kid, my bike meant independence.

Riding a bike in the mountains, however, was an entirely different experience. It was nothing like riding at sea level! At an elevation of sixty-five-hundred feet, there's a lot less oxygen to breathe. Just riding around the small loop in my neighborhood made my heart pound. I quickly realized that becoming a true mountain biker was going to be hard work. I was up for the challenge, but in order to learn how to *do* something, Tahoe-style, I had to start small. Really small. One of my biggest challenges was that I had become quite overweight after a hysterectomy, hormone treatments and the stress of going through a divorce.

I decided I'd challenge myself while no one was looking. My first goal was just to make it to the trail near my house, up a small hill. I got there! The view was perfectly stunning—a gently flowing

> I decided I'd challenge myself
> while no one was looking.

stream with a bridge over it, and the trail ambling off into the woods. Every day I challenged myself to go just a little bit further. Soon, I had learned to use all the gears on my bike. Power! One thing I learned very quickly about hills: When you go down, you have to go back up again. Another thing I learned: Momentum is your friend. I learned to zoom as fast as I could toward an incline with the gears in one and one—granny gear, they call it—and ride up very slowly, one pedal at a time.

One very steep incline I dubbed "Killer Hill," because I thought it was going to kill me every time I tried to ride up it! But I was determined to conquer it. On my first attempt, I had to get off my bike and walk it to the top. The second time I rode all the way to the top, but thought I was going to die. I felt as if my pounding heart was going to jump out of my chest. It was all I could do to keep from throwing up.

After a while, I could cover more interesting and difficult terrain. As I added more distance to my ride, I also added muscle and confidence. It took some time, but eventually I worked up to riding eighteen miles, up and down very steep terrain, through mountain trails in the high Sierra woods.

One day, I was riding on a trail and found myself in an oddly familiar place—beside an enormous boulder, which was warmed by the sun glinting over the blue lake. I was completely alone, yet I felt a sense of welcome. Then I remembered: When I'd first arrived in Tahoe, this was my special place to sit and meditate, to talk to God. I propped my bike against a Ponderosa pine and plunked myself down on the boulder. Feelings flooded back as I recalled how I made the decision to move here.

It was during a Fourth of July weekend. My soon-to-be-ex-husband and I had come to Tahoe for a last-ditch, save-the-marriage weekend. We watched the largest and most fantastic fireworks display over Lake Tahoe. I remembered the odd, detached feeling when the fireworks were over, and I remembered saying goodbye to my husband, who left the weekend early to go back to Florida. I was alone for the first time in twenty years, in this strange and beautiful place.

Mostly, though, I remembered winding up in a small local store for a pint of ice cream, my comfort food of choice. At the cash register, a local newspaper caught my eye, so I picked that up, too. I

> *One season—that's all it took to trans-form my life. You can transform, too.*

was scraping the bottom of the Double Chocolate Fudge in my hotel room when I noticed something in the paper—a career night on Tuesday at the Marriott Vacation Club. *Wait, Tuesday?* I thought. *When is Tuesday, anyway?* I actually had to call the resort operator to ask what day it was—that's how out of touch with reality I was.

It was Sunday. I had two days before the job fair. Enough time to call and get my name on the list, get my resumé organized and email it in. At the job fair, the whole situation felt surreal. Here I was in Lake Tahoe, applying for a job. What was I thinking? That I could just move here? Well, yes, apparently I did. It was a wild whim, out of the blue, but in the back of my mind I knew I was ready for change.

I was called in for an interview. And lo and behold, I got the job! The decision was made. I went back to Florida to pack up all my belongings, say goodbye to my husband and drive three-thousand miles to my new home all by myself. And now, sitting on the boulder, I realized I had done all this without ever looking back.

As I picked up my bike from the Ponderosa pine and headed back down the mountain, I felt something inside of me shift. I was evolving. Breath by breath, pedal by pedal, mile by mile, I was becoming someone—I was becoming *me*. And as the years passed in Tahoe, I witnessed changes. About every three or four months, the landscape went through slow yet profound alterations. As a Floridian, the concept of true seasonal change was alien to me.

The cycle of seasons gave me a sense of timing I'd never experienced before. Previously, my milestones were the ones I had arbitrarily created.

In Tahoe, people take advantage of everything they can do in each season because they know change is coming. I learned a deep lesson from these seasonal changes. Recognizing the changes helped me become clear on what I wanted to create in my life. This clarity enables me to live life to the fullest in each moment and each season of my life.

I realized that, being clear about what I truly wanted, I could create my own success. That realization led to my next venture: Success with Clarity, a system for personal, professional and business growth. Clarity allows us to become honest and open with ourselves and those around us. We acknowledge that we have contributed to changes in our lives that we didn't consciously intend to happen. We gain weight. We allow our finances to get out of control. We allow our relationships to deteriorate. These situations don't occur overnight, and they won't be corrected overnight either.

Once we decide we want to get on the path we *intend* for our lives, we often lack a clear vision of how to correct or right the situation. We don't really know how we got ourselves into the situation in the first place: *How the heck did I get here?* The truth is, we allowed ourselves to get out of control. The old saying that it's harder to turn a battleship than a small boat is true. Sometimes, we've been moving in the wrong direction so long that we don't know how to change course. The truth is that once you make the decision to take control of your life and get clear about what you truly want, success happens! One season—that's all it took to transform my life. You can transform, too.

Looking back, I've been practicing this principle my whole life. I've gradually made the changes that allow me to be my true self, who I authentically am. I believe anyone can do it—you don't have to move three-thousand miles to make it happen, either. Your dreams and adventures can start now, right where you are.

Go to a garden. Go to a theater. Or just go find a trail by your house. Your new adventure starts with deciding that you want something new. The key is getting clear about what you want and taking the right, first small step in the direction of your dream. It's probably right there, in your own backyard, waiting for you to take advantage of it!

Clare Dreyer, SPHR/founder, Success with Clarity, is a sought-after consultant, coach and inspirational speaker. She has more than twenty years' experience providing clients with a step-by-step strategic approach to catapulting forward in their business, professional or personal lives. Clare is now Assistant Director of Management and Leadership Programs for the Division of Extended Studies at the University of Nevada, Reno. Connect with Clare at www. SuccessWithClarity.com.

Marcy Cole, PhD

Into the Light

W hat is your essence? This was one of the first questions posed to each of us when we began the process of collaborating on this book. *Huh...I have no idea!* I have the capacity to see the true essence of others in, literally, a heartbeat. Yet after twenty years as a practicing psychotherapist, resolved to live my life on a conscious path, how was it that I was not in touch with this answer for myself?

Baffled and curious, I decided to excavate, and discover the true pulse of my life-force energy. While teaching a life enrichment class for women, I integrated an exercise into our evening together. We each wrote the question, "What is my essence?" with our dominant hands, then answered it with our non-dominant hands, which are said to bring forth creative flow and divine feminine guidance. Before my very eyes, the answer was reflected back to me in what looked like the scribbling of a preschooler: "I am a beacon of light."

What? A beacon? Who do you think you are? my internal voice said. *Your light's not always on!* I was struck by how quickly the critical judgments of my ego undermined what had been divinely revealed, reminding me of my core essence within as glimpsed through the lens of inspired self-reflection.

Recognizing myself as a "beacon of light" felt like a tall order, like a heavy, burdensome badge of honor. I clearly needed to research it further. I began by exploring how some definitions of this phrase carried metaphorical meaning in my life. The most common and ancient definition was of a lighthouse, guiding mariners to safe harbors and illuminating the shoals and rocks that could destroy their ships. The strength and focus of the beacon's beam is the product of its powerful lens and mirror.

Other descriptions included "guiding navigators to their destinations," "that which provides inspiration," "a source of light," "can see from a distance," and "a pole used as a standard or ensign set on the tops of mountains as a call to the people to assemble themselves for some great purpose." *YES. That's it!* This IS the energy field and intention that has resonated with and beckoned

> *Before my very eyes, the answer was reflected back to me in what looked like the scribbling of a preschooler: "I am a beacon of light."*

me my entire life. As the lighthouse stands, the beacon of light within me *has* provided guidance and support for others to focus their attention on their respective gifts, dreams and aspirations; it has championed their capacity to navigate their own journeys, and discover the light that shines within each one of them. Reflecting on this recognition, I see them—a sea of beautiful faces, faces of people with whom I've had the privilege of bearing witness to exquisite revelation and transformation.

I see Franny, a lovely, thirty-six-year-old Creole woman who was so convinced she looked like a monster that she would arrange her chair so that no one could see her profile, which she perceived as disfigured. Diagnosed with schizophrenia, chronic paranoid type, agoraphobia and body dysmorphic disorder, Franny had six psychiatric hospitalizations and had tried to commit suicide. She lived with a paralyzing and phobic fear of riding on buses and trains, and would not leave her house except to come to our appointments escorted by her caseworker. Her prior case notes suggested that, "Franny cannot tolerate much more than fifteen minutes of time per week. She'll get overwhelmed easily and will be ready to leave quickly." Despite these reports, I met with Franny for forty-five minutes every week for over four years.

During the initial phase of our work together, Franny's behavior was often childlike. She would push her chair away from me, and fidgeted with her hands. One of ten children, she felt "ugly" and was referred to by her family as "the stupid one." She was beaten

> *Reflecting on this recognition, I see them—a sea of beautiful faces, faces of people with whom I've had the privilege of bearing witness to exquisite revelation and transformation.*

regularly by her parents and older siblings and grew up feeling like a prisoner in her own home. Her punishments were severe. On one occasion she was made to kneel perfectly still on broken light bulbs while staring at a single lighted bulb on the ceiling.

She was scolded each time she looked away from her tormenter's eyes. During our sessions, her eyes never left mine. I listened. I mirrored back how hard her life had been for her. I educated her about how painful childhood messages and traumas can create false perceptions of ourselves and of others. By year two, her ruminations about her physical appearance began to lessen. She started to think, "Maybe, just maybe, I'm *not* the bad one." During year three, she began to express her authentic feelings rather than cling to the veil of her artificial smiles. She came out of seclusion, joining an outpatient partial-hospitalization program, where she interacted regularly with others.

In year four our sessions often took my breath away, as I witnessed this woman—who had been typecast as "chronically mentally ill"—break out of the barriers of her darkness and into the light of her desires. Throughout her life, she had believed that the locus of control was not within her power. I watched her begin to receive her worthiness and reclaim her power as she finally declared, "I am in charge of myself now." Franny began riding public transportation again, registered for classes at a community college and became interested in finding a job that suited her.

During our last session, I simply could not hold back the tears. Franny regressed a bit, saying, "It's me, isn't it?"

I reached out for her hand and said, "No, honey, these tears are not your fault. I am crying because I will miss you, and because it has been such a privilege to know you. You are an inspiration." She reached into her bag for a wrapped gift, a CD of love songs. As she walked down the hall she stopped and turned back to look at me, with an unforgettable expression that is etched in my heart's memory forever. Her eyes projected these words: "Thank you for seeing me."

Franny's story shows, so poignantly, how powerful it is when we begin to move into our light and recognize and embrace more of our true and divine nature. The years spent working with another client, Susan, also reminded me of our capacity to prevail against adversity and *choose* to live in the light of possibility.

I could feel Susan's gentle and loving spirit from the moment she entered my office, referred to me after a cocaine overdose. At nineteen, Susan looked haggard and felt hopeless, isolated and desperate for relief. On the edge of tears, she revealed her long-standing pattern of self-sabotage, expressing her feeling that she was defective and downright unlovable. Her story was fraught with consistent and cumulative pain, disappointment and neglect. Born to an abusive mother and abandoned by her biological father, Susan bounced around the foster care system. The verbal abuse she suffered during sporadic periods with her mother was some of the worst I'd ever heard. Her mother told her, "You're the abortion I *should* have had."

Despite numerous unsuccessful attachments and premature losses in her life, Susan committed herself to weekly sessions with me. Sometimes she wouldn't show up, but she would always come back ready to learn from the experiences she was hiding from. She always knew what needed attention—I simply held the space for her to feel heard, cared for unconditionally and seen for who she really is.

During the early stages of our working together, Susan got pregnant and decided to have the baby. It was the familial connection she had been longing for her whole life. Our work focused on helping her learn how to connect with *her* light within and shine it brightly upon herself and her child. As I talked to and cuddled and played with her darling baby Jackie, I could feel Susan's eyes studying my every move, and listening to my every word. She had never received this kind of nurturing in her entire life, and now she was responsible for caring for a child while still healing and finding her own ground.

A few years into our process, I left the counseling center and launched my own private practice. I gave Susan the option to continue to work with me at a reduced rate, or to work with a new therapist at the center. "I think I'll stay here," she announced. When I asked what inspired her decision she said, "Because I need to learn how to say 'goodbye' in a healthy way, instead of just running away." Susan had never had a safe place to land in relationships, and so she had never separated and moved on without unfinished business or unhealed wounds. Again I stood in awe of her courage and innate knowing of what she needed to experience for her own growth and highest good.

In the spring of 2010, fourteen years after our last visit, I received a note from Susan. Randomly surfing the television channels, she had seen me as a guest on CNN's sister station. I wept as I read her letter, brimming with gratitude for the time we had shared together and pride in her life today. She closed with, "During our process a hurt teenager grew into a woman, a wife and a loving mother of six." There is nothing sweeter than bearing witness to the strength of the human spirit as a wounded soul finds the voice of her heart, the light of her love and the joy of celebration.

I do not believe that life is about finding ourselves, but rather about remembering what we already know in order to fully embrace and express what we are here to share. Franny and Susan are but two of the dozens of individuals I have had the honor of accompanying on their journeys. But we are ALL really on the same journey, searching to recognize our own true essence and discover who we are apart from our past experiences and "stories." We all have our "Franny" moments of skewed self-perception, viewing ourselves as "disfigured" or somehow unworthy. And like Susan, we long to be loved and nurtured so we can acknowledge and amplify the light within and shine it upon others.

In mid-life, I recognized the power and beauty of the "beacon of light" energy that has and always will lie within me. Recognizing this allows me to shine brighter, offering others greater support to do so as well. Bearing witness to the divine light that lies within each one of us, which catapults us from darkness and despair into revelation and emancipation, is truly at the heart of my life's purpose and "essence." Of that, I am now certain.

So I encourage you to explore, discover and embrace *your* true essence. It will remind you who you are, and it will *always* be there to illuminate your way back… "into the light."

Marcy Cole, PhD, is a holistic psychotherapist, workshop facilitator, bestselling co-author and speaker. Over the last fifteen years, she has developed an extensive private practice with adults, couples and families, integrating Western and Eastern perspectives on achieving optimal health. She offers consultations at the Wheel of Well Being in Los Angeles, California, and by phone. Connect with Dr. Cole at www. DrMarcyCole.com.

Sajeela Cormack
You Are the Creator, Not the Created

In moments when we are pushed beyond our limits we can discover what our true capabilities are.

It was a cold, bright day on the farm when my family gathered to celebrate the christening of my eight-month-old son, Charlie. At the time, my older son, Hamish, was almost two and a half. It was time to feed the farm animals, and my dad asked if anyone would like to come along. All the grandchildren and parents called out, "Yes!" Dad directed them to the carryall on the back of tractor.

Hamish and I came later, as I was getting a jacket for him. Hamish ran to be picked up by his Parpie, with me hot on his tail. I picked him up to put him in his grandfather's arms. As Parpie leaned over to take him, his foot slipped on the clutch. The tractor jumped forward, knocking Hamish out of my arms to the ground, and sending me flying backward.

In shock, my father quickly put his foot back on the clutch, and it slipped again. The tractor jumped again, and suddenly half of Hamish's body was underneath the back tire. Desperate and panicky, my father put his foot back onto the clutch. It slipped yet again. The tractor jumped and stalled. Hamish's entire body was now beneath the back tire, his head pinned to one side.

It happened in a couple of minutes. I had read stories of women performing amazing feats of strength when their children were in danger. In fright, I tried to lift the tractor off my son. But I couldn't. I watched Hamish's eyes pop and his face go blue. Desperate, I ran to the front of the tractor, trying to lift it again. Then I ran, screaming, "No! No, not now! Please dear God, not now!"

I had just watched my son die.

My brother saw my distress, raced after me and held me tightly. I looked over and saw they had lifted my son from under the tractor—my then-husband was holding Hamish's limp body. He was dead. Suddenly, I became still and calm and enormous power

You are the creator, not the created.

came through me—a strong connection to the Earth and Universe. I pried my brother's arms open and moved with massive speed and agility through the fence to Hamish. I felt something inside me saying, *"Shake your son! Shake him!"* My husband swore at me in panic as I quickly and briefly shook Hamish with the electric current moving through my hands... he took a breath. I said, "Sit him up! Sit him up!" And we sat him upright.

Hamish is alive today. He's thirty-one, now. At six feet, six and a half inches tall, and a beautiful man, Hamish has lived a fulfilling life. I never have and never will forget that day. In that moment when my hands touched him, I experienced an incredible force that is unparalleled—I became part of it. I was so still and focused, without any stress, and yet I was immensely powerful. I became the observer of, and a participant in, a connection to a greater power that enabled me to bring life to another human being.

The change this brought in *me* was monumental. In that moment of crisis, I became an entirely different woman. Watching my son die and come back to life shifted my own life into an amazing state of gratitude. I had inner strength that I'd not felt before. It was clear to me from that day onward that whatever I dreamed of doing, I could do. Before then, my marriage had been in an unhealthy place. I felt that I was a victim, with no choices in my life. The life-changing experience with Hamish showed me that I had more capacity than I ever thought and that I had the freedom to choose my circumstances.

I believe this is what being a transformational woman is about. It's calling upon Universal power in moments you feel you have no way to achieve what you want to. My mission and all of the work that I do with speaking, consulting and writing is to open people up to the possibility and field of intelligence that surrounds them and exists within, and awaken them to their true potential.

You are the creator, not the created. Most people believe that they are the created, not the creator—but it's not true. In every moment you *do* have a choice—a choice that's available twenty-four hours a day, in every second, to go deeper into the divine intelligence of the Universe. You are spirit, and through taking

You are the power that you dream of.

accountability for your own life across all areas—cleaning up your being through healthy, conscious eating and living, meditation, enjoyment and adventure—you can live a magnificent existence.

Five core principles allow me to feel inspired and to be inspirational, which is another quality of being a transformational woman and leader. First, I choose to live a life in connection with the divine in which I embrace possibilities and know I can create what I love. Second, I treat my body as a temple by consuming live, fresh, healthy and unprocessed foods from local sources. Third, I get clear on, and ask for, what I want by following my heart and intuition and never giving up.

Being authentic, having fun, keeping things simple and being grateful is the fourth principle of being a transformational woman. And fifth, I continue working with empowered and empowering people who are also focused on their mission and destiny.

You are the power that you dream of. Since that time almost thirty years ago, I have felt that same tremendous power move me on many occasions. I have miraculously and instantaneously healed my own body. Every day I live a conscious, authentic life of spiritual commitment and deep love. I practice trusting myself, my intuition and others faster, and I see that everything is in divine order, no matter how tough, conflicting or challenging a situation may be.

I remind myself and invite you to remember: You are not separate from the bigger picture of life. Make the choice to be the illuminated and the illuminator for those around you. Harness the inner leader and know that you have tremendous power to make a difference in the world.

> *You have choice in every moment of your life. You have the choice to take your life from where it is to where you'd love it to be.*

Most of us have had trust beaten out of us by parental and societal conditioning. We put on masks and shields to protect ourselves, losing sight of who we innately are. Whenever there is love present, there is the ability to trust. When there is trust, there is no fear—they can't occupy the same space. When we trust, we can open ourselves up to see other perspectives.

The five core principles I practice will assist you to live a circular life—joy-filled, reaction-free and free of emotional and physical pain. From this awakened perspective, you can affirm to yourself: *I am the creator of my WHOLE reality.* Being a creator means you have the power to love and nurture yourself in the seven areas of life: health and fitness, family and relationships, career, finances, spirituality, fun and adventure, personal growth and development and giving back. You deserve to do so.

What can you do to live as the creator? You can change your internal language—self-talk—from negative to empowering. You can meet with yourself every day, whether through yoga, sitting on the beach or under a tree, or watching your breath in meditation. You can be a part of nature—it speaks, if you're willing to listen. In stillness, new options become available to you. The Universal truths and laws are all around you, showing you ways to stay connected and giving you the confidence to know that you are one with the incredible magnificence that you see all around you, and that *you* are that magnificence. You have choice in every moment of your life. You have the choice to take your life from where it is to where you'd love it to be.

The story of my son Hamish is an example of the invisible power that lies within each one of us—this inner power enables us to have that choice to change. I was given a gift. I realized that we actually have access to infinite energy in every moment. I believe that we are too conditioned so that we live in fear, doubt, and under the assumption that we are the effect rather than the cause of life.

After experiencing firsthand the true capacity of what we all have inside, I can never go back to believing that I, or anyone else, is less powerful than I was in that moment of pure love when I called my son back to life. We are alchemists by nature: constantly transforming, changing, growing, evolving.

My message is about bringing awareness to action, creating a gap between stimulus and response so that you choose your responses, instead of reacting blindly and uncontrollably. Practicing these skills empowers you to make choices that positively support you and your life. After all I have experienced, I am certain that the Universe is there to help you achieve what you dream, and I believe that it is our birthright to do it, and *be* transformational women for the world.

Sajeela Cormack is an international bestselling author, speaker and holistic gourmet raw food chef and consultant. She is a contributing author to many cookbooks and three international bestselling books. Sajeela is committed to making raw food a way of life by her simple and fun approach to fantastic health. The host and producer of the television show God's Garden, Sajeela is an authority on eating raw super foods and healing your body naturally.

Sajeela has also successfully started and sold several companies. She brings a wealth of knowledge and understanding not only to day-to-day business operations, but also to the economic strategies needed to create hyper-growth for any organization. Connect with Sajeela at www.SajeelaCormack.com.

Albertine Phan

In the Power of
Your Stillness: First,
Do No Harm

The best-kept secrets are revealed to me on Tuesdays. On these transcendent days, I walk among the shadows of the Downtown Eastside (DTES) of Vancouver, the poorest postal code in Canada. Behind the walls of this city, miracles happen. Many here grew up in a cacophony of anger, chaos, frustration, violence, abuse and neglect. In their pain and alienation, they turned to substance misuse and so live with their shadows. They are the keepers of all the secrets of human experience we so often choose to ignore. And yet, as we've worked together to move past the limitations of addiction, I have seen such strength, such profound life force shining through in their eyes.

After each experience of seeing a client connect with that force and reclaim the ability and power to co-create the choices she wants, I feel even deeper gratitude for my life. It is an incredible gift I've been handed, to be in a place to help cultivate—and bear witness to—the animating spirit that, at the core of our beings, inhabits and guides us all when given the chance. I gather strength from the stories I hear and count my blessings while all around me tremendous transformations take place.

If you had asked me at age four what I wanted to be when I grew up, I would have answered, "A fairy godmother and an astronaut." I wanted to be a fairy godmother because I dreamed of making peoples' greatest desires a reality; and I wanted to be an astronaut because I thought, *What better way is there to travel and visit people on other planets?* Of course, I had a very fertile imagination.

As a child, I had a glandular problem for which my mom eventually brought me to the hospital. The surgeon came out of the operating room to meet us in his dirty gown, covered in blood. When I saw him I got scared and immediately thought: Nobody *is going to touch me or cut me open.* I willed myself to get better,

> *I gather strength from the stories I hear and count my blessings while all around me tremendous transformations take place.*

and did. By the time I was in fifth grade, I added doctor-healer-magician to my repertoire of future occupations. I wanted to be someone who could help people get better without causing them further harm.

At about the same time, my father died, leaving many issues unresolved and activating what became a long struggle with depression for me. In my depression, I did not grieve the loss of my father—who in many subtle ways shaped my relationship to the world.

But somehow, in my father's absence and in the midst of my mother's own grief and depression, my belief in magic kept beating strong in those chambers of my heart where innocence remained untouched—and ready to play when the time was right.

It wasn't until my late twenties that I started appreciating my father. Memories of a serious disciplinarian, a man of few words who had little time for play and always seemed annoyed by my questions, dissipated, replaced by memories of the man who encouraged my creativity and imagination. I thought of my father's passion for clouds, and the interminable hours we spent resting on thick pillows of moss gazing up at them, my imagination running wild at the sight of big fluffy bunnies or the simple beauty of a rainbow.

During that time of reckoning, I also found a homeopath who guided me out of my depression, and I continued to work on it during my four years in homeopathy school. My childhood encounter with the surgeon had planted a seed for this lifelong pursuit, and it opened me to my passion for true love and inner peace. In learning, practicing and applying all that the gentle arts of energetic healing have to offer, I gave my soul an opportunity for full creative expression, and I found a sense of purpose and belonging.

Homeopathic treatment gently realigned my body, mind and spirit to function as one, again, with the unconditional life force of love and creativity. In the process, it reintroduced me to magical thinking. I allowed my imagination to take over, and created something outside of my circumstances. When I let myself get lost in the clouds again, take the good from my childhood and become strong enough to leave the agonizing cycle of self-destruction and

> *This was my natural way of being. I had simply forgotten to nurture it.*

defeat, the truth of my self emerged: I finally knew I was one with all life, and learned to embrace it with joy, ease and the experience of true unconditional love. This was my natural way of being. I had simply forgotten to nurture it.

At its core, healing is all about listening to and relating to a person as a singular and intelligent being, so it is unique in its respect for the individual. What makes you, *you?* That is the central guiding question. When I was first invited to practice homeopathy in a detox clinic and women's residence in the DTES of Vancouver, the first moment I sat down with a client, something settled in my body. After a few seconds of pure silence—that eternity present in epiphany—I knew: *My own life experience was preparation to do this work. It's what I was meant to do.* The philosophy of all the energy-based medicines I studied became a lifestyle for me: First, do no harm.

Results in my first month were astonishing. People who had been plagued by night terrors—rendering them exhausted and afraid to sleep—were able to sleep peacefully through the night for the first time in years. Others cut back significantly on antidepressants, sleeping pills and pain medication. In the absence of heavy sedation, they developed a better sense of their own feelings and sensations. They, too, saw that gentle stimulation to the life force *can* peacefully realign the body, the mind and the spirit and bring it into oneness with the infinite power of the universal life force.

Never in my wildest dreams would I have conceived of such a triumph. Little me with my wild imagination, able to effect profound changes for people! I felt like a fairy godmother, using the tools on hand combined with the will and understanding to choose: a great recipe for inner peace. I guess dreams do come true.

> *Your life force and the entire universe are invested to support you.*

One man I treated was on the verge of suicide when he first arrived. After the first six weeks, he said, "I never thought I would say or feel this, but I really feel like I've regained my faith in humanity." Through my own life experience, and witnessing my clients, I have learned that we are each innately built to survive. Our immune systems and will to live can and do transcend layers of negative belief and perception.

The extraordinary transformations I witness in my practice have shown me that part of my purpose is to share that my love of life, my joy for the gift of life and this incredible opportunity to create beauty and possibilities, will never ever and *can* never ever be taken away from me—least of all by me, because I decided that being in the joy and love of life are my greatest acts of defiance in the face of any adversity, limitation or sorrow.

The fact that rain is wet cannot be changed. Appreciating the clouds for their power to sustain life and set us to dreaming is just a matter of perspective.

My clients tell me that yoga, meditation and homeopathy are so powerful in the recovery process because these practices give them a sense of inner peace. Inner peace is the greatest possible contribution you can make to peace on the planet. Peace begins within *you*. Your life force and the entire universe are invested to support you.

The first thing to do on this path to peace is to learn how to breathe. Calm the breath, and you calm the mind. The calmer your mind is, the more space you create for what exists in the moment. In stillness, breath will always bring you back to yourself, your body, your own moment of true presence. Everything grows from allowing this space within to just be. The deeper you breathe, the more you live. Each breath inspired creates life, and this is where healing begins.

Everyone has dreams, and everyone gets stuck in the shadows sometimes. But you have the power to emerge, take charge of yourself with gentleness and compassion and shine with your own life force. You are the source of your own power. May you listen, and remember.

For more than half her life, Albertine Phan has practiced and applied to her own health what she has learned from energetic medicine modalities such as Reiki, pranic healing, classical homeopathy, yoga and the One Brain Method in her effort to serve the full actualization of human potential for the highest good of all. Albertine was invited as a Pathway to Peace delegate at the United Nations for the Commission on the Status of Women as a supporter of the 5th World Conference on Women (5wcw.org). Albertine is also a core instrumental leader in "Get Your Woman On!" Connect with Albertine at www.SwitchedOnHealth.com.

Mia-Michelle Henry

The Courage to Forgive

I shouted angrily at God as I sat in my car outside the restaurant. "Why shouldn't I punch him in the nose? He deserves it!" Two memories flooded back; the first was Paul's beautiful blue eyes looking at me with love and adoration when we first met, and the second was the sound of Paul's voice on the phone when he told me he was abandoning his unborn son… and me.

And now here I was, twenty-two years later, parked outside the restaurant where Paul and I were to meet—and all I could think about was how good it would feel to punch him in the nose when I saw him.

I met Paul when I was eighteen. I was wide-eyed, adventure-loving and ready to change the world. He was handsome, tall and confident, and his strong Dutch accent was charming. He had the most beautiful blue eyes I had ever seen, filled with promise. He was very hard to resist. We became friends and soon fell in love. And suddenly, with my first love, I was living my dream: traveling the globe and performing with the international organization "Up With People."

Everything changed for both of us when I found out I was pregnant. We were scared, but we were also excited. This would simply be another chapter in our adventure and life together. However, Paul's father was having none of it. He encouraged Paul to leave me. He thought Paul was too young for fatherhood, and he didn't want his son taken away by an American girl. In his mind, getting me pregnant was a mistake.

I remember the day as if it was yesterday. I was eight months pregnant, and had been waiting for Paul in the States. He would return for the birth and then take us back to the Netherlands. My phone rang. "I'm not coming to get you," Paul said from the other line. I waited for him to explain. Nothing but silence.

"When will you be coming, then?" I asked in confusion. "Never," he answered flatly. It still didn't compute. "Why?" I asked. "I don't love you anymore." And he hung up. Brhy, our son, was born two weeks later.

"When will you be coming, then?" I asked in confusion.

"Never," he answered flatly. It still didn't compute.

"Why?" I asked.

"I don't love you anymore." And he hung up. Brhy, our son, was born two weeks later.

I was stunned. Paralyzed. My entire world instantly crumbled around me. I had invested everything in this man, in our future together. He was my soul mate, my first—and what I thought would be my last—love. I thought he was the doorway to my dreams. And now he was gone without any apparent reason. I was heartbroken. My two choices were to collapse or to keep moving. It took all the strength I had, but I chose the latter. After Brhy was born, I poured myself into him. He became my life and my love.

It was a struggle, but I was determined to make it. However, over the next seven years I sometimes punished myself for my shortcomings and felt resentful for my dashed dreams and my lost love. I felt angry, bitter and stuck. I finally found my strength in prayer. It became the transformative force in my life and the path to everything good that happened after my abandonment. I prayed for wisdom and strength. I prayed for healing for me, for Brhy and for Paul.

Prayer taught me how to forgive myself for all my faults, all my shortcomings. It peeled away the layers of anger and resentment I had toward Paul and laid bare the true love that was always there. Prayer guided me. Prayer freed me. Prayer enhanced me. It made me the person who was ready to be loved. And that's when my true soul mate and present-day husband, Wesley, came into my life.

Wesley was there through the aftershock of my abandonment years. Supporting me, adoring me, forgiving me, allowing me to bloom into who I am today. Eventually we married. He welcomed Brhy as his own son, and Brhy accepted him as his father. In the fifteen years since then, we have had three more children and built a life together. And through it all, we prayed. We learned to forgive each other for our imperfections. I realized I had much to offer the world. My relationship with God deepened, grew more intimate. I went back to school, completed my Master's. I continued my life of service, teaching others to heal as I had done.

And then, from out of the blue, Paul called again. He wanted a relationship with his son. My son needed it as well, and had asked me to be okay with his need to know his biological father. So here I was, sitting in my car, parked outside the restaurant where I was to meet Paul. And all I wanted to do was punch him in the nose. My entire life seemed to be converging on this one moment.

So I said a final prayer to God. I said, "God, I don't want to do what I want to do, out of my own personal anger. I want to do what *you* want me to do. Direct my words, direct my actions. Help me find the calm and the stillness in my heart." I took a deep breath and went inside the restaurant. Paul was sitting alone in a booth. He looked so much older, so much smaller than I remembered. I sat down across from him. He took a deep breath and fixed his blue eyes on me. "Can you forgive me?" he asked.

I looked into his face. It was the same face, the same eyes. He had some wrinkles where there had never been any before, but I saw something more; where once there had been love and confidence in his eyes, now there was only pain and regret. Suddenly, I realized: "What do I have to be angry about? I was allowed to keep and raise my son. I met my soul mate and loving, adoring husband, Wesley, and now I have three more beautiful children. Every day I am affecting people's lives positively. I am loved. I love. I have an amazing life."

But it was different for Paul. Here was a man filled with guilt and shame wanting to see the son he had abandoned, facing the woman he had wronged—facing the greatest mistake of his life.

I took a deep breath and said to him, "Paul, I forgave you a long time ago. Now I need you to do something for me. You have to forgive yourself." And I watched twenty years of regret lift from his

> *I took a deep breath and said to him, "Paul, I forgave you a long time ago. Now I need you to do something for me. You have to forgive yourself." And I watched twenty years of regret lift from his eyes.*

eyes. But even beyond this, I felt a sudden exhilaration. The closure was so powerful. My heart, the heart that had been broken twenty-two years ago, was now fully healed. We were like old friends, talking like it was yesterday, talking about our families, our work and our shared passions. The wall between us had crumbled.

A short time after this meeting, I was asked to give a speech to a group of people. The topic: *Who are you?* I confided in a friend, "I don't know who I am anymore! Who am I?" I was filled with so many conflicting emotions, I just didn't know.

My friend smiled and said to me, "You are the essence of love. Who else would sit and look a man in the face who had left her and her child? Who else could survive alone with that child and then twenty-two years later come back and forgive that same man? That is love. You are love!"

People often ask me what my greatest achievement is. I tell them, my relationship to God. It is the foundation for all my other relationships. But how does one initiate this relationship with God? First, you have to understand that a power exists that is greater than yourself. Whatever the name, God or Creator, it doesn't matter. You have to surrender to the fact that there is a God. Prayer is our way of talking to that creator, the way that we build a relationship.

If we all prayed in this way, we would learn to move beyond ourselves and begin to serve the greater good. Healing begins on

> *Prayer is a tool for transformation—for individuals and for nations. It is the first thing. The essential thing. The building block toward peace in yourself and on this planet.*

the most intimate levels, between friends and family, between husband and wife; but it can grow toward the larger community, between neighbors and towns and nations. Forgiveness has to start with our selves, one person at a time, but it doesn't need to stop there. Its power is limitless. Prayer is a tool for transformation—for individuals and for nations. It is the first thing. The essential thing. The building block toward peace in yourself and on this planet.

Prayer is simply the activity of talking to God. Most people use prayer to get something that they want, as a self-serving tool. But its more profound purpose is to develop a deeper relationship with God, whether in giving thanks, seeking wisdom or guidance, asking help for others or dealing with loss and death. Prayer is the bridge to forming a unique intimacy with your personal creator. It is the purest communication. It doesn't have to be pretty or formal or even solemn; it can be argumentative, challenging, messy. Prayer is where true authenticity lives, where you can learn who you really are and truly *be*.

Prayer and forgiveness helped me find the courage to direct my own life. It allowed me to find peace in my heart over Paul's abandonment. It allowed me the strength to forgive him, and in turn allowed him to begin to forgive himself. It allowed me to re-embrace the love we once had, the love that created our beautiful son, Brhy. That true love was finally given the honor it deserved. Ultimately, prayer and forgiveness transformed me into the person I needed to be to attract the things that I wanted, and the life I was meant to live.

It can do the same for you.

Mia-Michelle Henry is a transformational life coach, educator, trainer and Les Brown Platinum speaker. Her expertise is in relationships; her passion is to help children process grief and loss; and her life's work is to bring a message of love and encouragement to people around the world. With a strong spiritual center, Mia-Michelle continues to serve humanity with her gifts and talents. Connect with Mia-Michelle at www.MiaMichelle.com and www.AuthenticHearts.com.

Michele A. Wilson
Achieve Your Dreams – Have a Plan B

O ctober 15, 2009: My six-year-old son, Jovaan, becomes seriously ill and is rushed to University of California Los Angeles Children's Hospital. Life as we know it totally changes, and our home is now in his hospital room as we wait for weeks—and then months—for his diagnosis and recovery.

I can't even begin to describe the pain and suffering Jovaan goes through. After weeks of invasive testing and much head-shaking by doctors, he is finally diagnosed with a rare disease called Chronic Intestinal Pseudo-Obstruction (CIP). Though there is no actual blockage in his intestines, his body is behaving as if there is. Jovaan has all the worst symptoms: pain, food aversion, diarrhea, constipation and weight loss. I am told that there is no cure for his illness.

I don't know how long we will be in the hospital. Day after day, hour after hour, doctors and nurses file in and out of the room, performing tests and keeping the IVs going. Nothing they try yields results that they consider normal. I set up a bed for myself in the room and try to work, but I miss deadlines and can't make meetings. For the first time in my life, I can't do the work I've promised to do. As a single mom, I'm the breadwinner. I have a car payment coming up. Insurance is due. If I don't work, my bills won't be paid—and then how will I take care of my kids?

I have great support from family and friends, but all of them have very busy lives. Even though they come to visit and give me breaks, at some point they have to leave. I don't want Jovaan to ever be alone. And I need to be fully present for him as an advocate as well as a loving mom. He has several teams of great doctors, but there are definitely times I have to speak up and say, "This is not working. We need to stop."

One night, early on in our hospital stay, I hear a little child crying and screaming, "Please don't leave me, Mom! Please don't leave me!" It breaks my heart to hear him begging her to stay, knowing that she probably has no choice but to go. All over the hospital, patients are alone without spouses or family members to

> *Though I am out on a limb, the choice is clear: I have to be with my son, whatever happens. I will not leave his side. I have to come up with a Plan B right away.*

hold their hands, talk to them, comfort them. On our floor, even babies are left alone. The sacrifice seems necessary—but I know it shouldn't be. *It is wrong for people to have to make such a choice.*

The choice before me, too, is to be present at the hospital to love, protect and advocate for my child, or to leave him alone in order to make the money necessary to keep a roof over our heads. Though I am out on a limb, the choice is clear: I have to be with my son, whatever happens. I will not leave his side. I have to come up with a Plan B right away.

I had big dreams when I was growing up. Dancing was my passion, and I wanted to be a professional. At the age of seventeen, I became a single mother, and my dreams slipped away—but I was lucky to be given great parents who were very caring and loving and who taught me strong Christian family values. My mom and dad always empowered and supported me. "Focus on what you can do, not what you can't," they said. Even when I had my first child in high school, they encouraged me to graduate and go to college.

It took me ten years to complete college, but even with my degree in hand, I worked multiple jobs and couldn't afford the rent. At the age of forty-three, I found myself divorced and struggling, a single mom with three children, no place to live, no job and no car. I was forced to move back in with my parents. Instead of looking at my life as a failure, I turned to God for wisdom and guidance. I began to make my journey of personal development and to investigate my purpose in life. And, I made my first life plan.

As I started to rebuild my life in the business world, I determined that my passion was to help small business owners and entrepreneurs grow and refine their businesses. I had worked in the banking, insurance, real estate and Internet industries in various management positions, and I started several part-time businesses. Although I had struggled, my diverse experiences were the blessing that equipped me to launch a new business designed to support small business owners.

During this time, I had health issues and suddenly became alarmed: I was a single mom without a will. If something happened to me, my young son could become a ward of the court and possibly be placed into foster care. A good friend showed me her company's services; they could take care of all of my legal needs, and affordably. I enrolled in a membership. She also told me about wealth-creating opportunities available to those who signed others up for memberships. The system sounded easy to follow and did not depend on my skills or background to be successful. It depended on just one thing: my willingness to be coached. At the hospital with Jovaan, I called my friend in desperation. "I'm here for the foreseeable future," I said. "I have a laptop, a cell phone and a burning desire to succeed. Tell me what to do."

Suddenly, the concept of making residual income seemed obvious and very, very important. In my situation, I had no choice but to leverage my income. And why not? I could market a product and service I really believed in—I could make a living and still make a difference. Most importantly, it would allow me to stay in the hospital with my son.

So I dove into my Plan B and created a whole new business from our tiny hospital room. I set up my office there, complete with laptop and printer, and decorated the walls with banners, balloons, letters and pictures from children in Jovaan's class. Among the flowers and toys from his fans—big and small—were my various papers and office supplies.

To my surprise, I discovered that I truly loved my work. Before, I always traded time for money, doing things I didn't really care about. Now I felt truly inspired. I even got promoted while in the hospital!

My new business partners were amazing. With so many doctors caring for Jovaan, I never knew when they might come in. So when I had to make a business call, I got other team members on three-

> *At the hospital with Jovaan, I called my friend in desperation. "I'm here for the foreseeable future," I said. "I have a laptop, a cell phone and a burning desire to succeed. Tell me what to do."*

way calls with me. Then I'd simply put my phone on mute and have them take over when I needed to be there for my son. In quiet moments, I was able to put everything else into place, bringing in new business partners to join my team while residually boosting my own income. All of this took place over several months in a hospital room.

As much as he suffered, Jovaan was always brave, and such a happy, positive child. I learned so much from him: courage, hope, perseverance and the power of prayer. Even after two major surgeries, he smiled and laughed and told me, "Don't worry, Mom. I will be okay."

Nurses often remarked, "How wonderful that you can stay with Jovaan in the hospital this whole time! We know it helps with his healing process." I could feel that, too. Jovaan's attitude made every day a blessing. How blessed I was to be there! And how blessed I am to be here at home with him now, able to enjoy his improved health and continue to help him heal.

It is so important to create a Plan B—you never know what might happen. And life should not demand that anyone trade what is really important in order to make money. Creating different income streams, especially residual ones, is key for anyone who is looking for a deeper quality of life.

> *Make a one-year plan, a two-year plan, a five-year plan and a ten-year plan. If you change your mind, it's okay. Build a new life plan, a Plan B.*

However you find your passion and income, the first step toward the kind of independence I discovered from my son's hospital room is creating a life plan, just as you would a business plan. Many businesses skip this crucial step and fail. Life needs a plan, just as businesses do; and you can create a life plan easily, based on the structure of a business plan.

Write down your life vision and mission statements and determine your core values—who and what you want to be. Determine what you're great at. Next, surround yourself with likeminded people, such as family members, friends, personal or professional life coaches and mentors, who will support your dreams. Then structure your life so that you can work a little bit, every day, toward making your dream happen. Just don't let your work work *you*.

I sit down every month and draw up a plan for the following month. And each night I make a plan for the next day. If I don't get everything done, I allow tasks to carry over without guilt. One plan feeds into the larger cycle, and the next and, before I know it, I've accomplished something I once never dreamed I was capable of. Make a one-year plan, a two-year plan, a five-year plan and a ten-year plan. If you change your mind, it's okay. Build a new life plan, a Plan B.

Working not just to survive, but to give back—whether through charity, building community or making art—is crucial for our hearts and souls, and for the rest of the world. Now that my business is full-steam ahead, my goal is to create one hundred millionaires who will be in position to make great contributions. One of my greatest passions is working with Get Your Woman On, a social network and forum for women committed to collaborative success and to transforming the quality of the lives of women on the planet.

The more financial freedom we have, the more the cycle of giving back expands. Our choices expand. Free from the live-to-work paradigm, we are free to help each other, and to spend time on what is most important—like being with our children.

Michele Alyce Wilson is a single mom, an entrepreneur, a Small Business & Group Specialist with Go Small Biz & Pre-Paid Legal Services, Inc., and Chief Business Development Officer (CBDO) with Get Your Woman On (www.GetYourWomanOn.com). She has a BS in business management. Drawing on more than twenty years of experience in corporate management, Michele assists entrepreneurs and small and home-based business owners around the globe with strategic planning, systems development and day-to-day operations so they can focus on their families and on the business of making money. Michele is also a grassroots advocate for children with GI conditions through the International Foundation for Functional Gastrointestinal Disorders (IFFGD). Connect with Michele at www.MicheleWilsonInternational. com.

Lorraine Francis

Sustainable Joy

C onsider the word *joy.*
    On paper my life looked fantastic. I'm a highly successful female entrepreneur, an award-wining architect and a happy wife and mother. For most of my life, I had not given the word much thought. But one night, at a women's circle, each of us were asked to pick a word out of a cloth bag to carry us forward. I drew my word: Joy.

I thought I was supposed to get some power word, some wisdom word—when I got that little word, I was disappointed. I thought, What do I need this for? In the moment, I assumed I already had joy. I'm a happy person, always smiling, and overall, yes, life was pretty incredible! So what was this part of me that couldn't stop thinking about joy? A question formed: *Was I really feeling it?* I tried stepping outside myself and asking again, asking my heart: *Are you feeling joy?*

The answer was no. And when I realized that, I saw just how essential joy really is. It took strength and courage to dig within and sit with the sadness of realizing joy didn't live in my heart.

Why was I unsatisfied? Why was I settling for less than joy? Something inside me wanted to be free, but I wanted one-hundred-percent perfect. I was constantly striving, looking into the future. Concerned with big plans and dreams, I was moving too fast out of the present. I belittled my achievements, struggled with confidence and felt under-entitled to live a big, beautiful life. I lacked balance between family and career, always choosing one or the other rather than choosing myself. Ultimately, this led to self-sabotage.

Self-examination showed me that what I really needed was to slow down and enjoy myself while doing the work of living—to stop for a second, give myself a big pat on the back and say, *Wow! You're doing great. Take a deep breath, suck this in and really live it.* Then we got an English bulldog, one of the slowest dogs in the world. He brought me back down to earth, helped to shift my perspective and slowed me down when I wanted to sprint ahead. I started to ground myself.

Joy is being present in the moment, and it can't really be experienced outside the moment. When you ask yourself, Am I joyful? *you are, ironically, pushing joy aside. You're already on to the next thing.*

The more I softened and quieted my movement, moving to center and listening to my heart, the more I recognized that joy isn't somewhere in the future. And it doesn't mean being (or having) perfection. Being a type A perfectionist overachiever had brought me many things, but joy was not one of them.

Joy is being present in the moment, and it can't really be experienced outside the moment. When you ask yourself, Am I joyful? you are, ironically, pushing joy aside. You're already on to the next thing. Joy is a state of mind. It's about connecting to the authentic self. No part of the self wants to be blocked or denied— that only creates conflict and dis-ease.

As a professional woman in a man's world, I always had to wear a mask of sorts to show I was worthy of respect. I went to engineering school at the age of eighteen and was the only woman in my class of forty, and even these days I don't find myself sitting across from too many other women architects.

So I never hung around many women, until I joined the circle. The support for each woman's growth in that space was phenomenal. It showed me what true feminine power is capable of when we work together to find sustainable solutions.

My new bonds with women have supported me in creating more joy and laughter in my life and not taking the world so seriously. Getting together with other women is so important for creating real joy and success, and it has helped soothe my tumultuous inner world.

It also showed me there were parts of myself I'd willfully blocked. Throughout my career, I've worn the pants. Making tough decisions with a lot of men present meant denying my feminine self on some level and buying into the masculine view that joy is based on "success" rather than inner strength, harmony and emotional stability. Sometimes, I'd deliberately make the decision to walk into a meeting as a male.

So when I asked myself about joy, I knew a big part of getting in touch with it and making it sustainable was expressing my whole being, including the femininity I'd always stifled to be "strong." That meant making time for self-care and nurturing, including getting my eyebrows waxed or taking walks on the beach that I had denied because of my "busy" calendar. Allowing myself these pleasures, and saying more noes to others while saying more yeses to myself, helped bring me out of my monkey mind and back to the present.

I wanted to be one person, in one body. I wanted my business and private selves to be in alignment. So I tried it. And I found that it puts me at ease. I stopped having stress stomachaches and waking in the middle of the night thinking about my to-do list. I noticed it put others around me at ease, too. It was magical—when I expressed my authentic self, suddenly everyone loosened up and all the masks came off. And I have not paid a price in terms of lack of respect. I do what I need to do to own the space. I can still command a boardroom when necessary—and I can be joyful and feminine when I do.

Now, at a time when many are losing hope and living in fear, my life is expanding from my core of inner peace and sustained well-being. I've always wanted to make a big difference in the sustainability of our planet and help more women and children— our future change agents—and now it's all showing up, with bigger players. I don't have to do it all by myself.

So how do we start from joy? I've seen many other women struggling, rushing, achieving, multi-tasking and sacrificing themselves. For what? We can use our natural grace as women to achieve our true greatness, which I believe is connecting with our joy. But first we've got to slow down and give ourselves room to breathe and connect with what's happening all around us. The

> *Sustainable joy lies in appreciating even the imperfect, even the totally frustrating, moment.*

moment you allow this, you're in the moment. Notice this and breathe it in. Quiet your mind and connect with your heart. Joy means *right now*.

Rather than just running the to-do list and crossing things off, try waking up each morning and asking this essential question, stopping to wait for a response: *What's in MY highest good today?* Sometimes it takes a few minutes to hear the true answer to this question, but it will come. Nature is a great place to do this. When you need to ground yourself and enter the present, go somewhere quiet and beautiful—under a tree, by a lake, on a mountain or in a lovely room that feels like a sanctuary. Tap into the quiet. Feel it in all your cells. Your subconscious will let you know if you are aligned, in joy, with your goals.

Sustainable joy lies in appreciating even the imperfect, even the totally frustrating, moment. Starting from joy is an essential component in any transformational experience. So take your joy back! Embrace yourself at your core. Listen to and trust your intuition. You don't have to carry your past baggage, situations or stories. You can decide today whatever you want to be true. You will be provided for. If you move from joy and a clear intention, your goals show up for you.

In my research, I've seen that few women have done over one million dollars in business revenue per year. In the past, I achieved this level and more doing things the hard way. I'd like to see women

> *Joy makes you available to the world in a sustainable way—thereby fostering sustainability in the world.*

with more plans, more tools, more financing and bigger businesses, so that collectively we can make a difference for ourselves and our ailing planet. With all the support out there, the missing link is authenticity. We need the harmony that comes from joy to create it and stand tall within ourselves.

Joy makes you available to the world in a sustainable way— thereby fostering sustainability in the world. The presence and participation of joyful women is required to make the giant leaps needed for overall sustainability. More women at the table, working in collaboration, will create waves of innovation, whether it's decreasing our carbon footprint or fighting disease. There is no need to be fearful, guilty, overworked or overburdened. Let's surrender to joy and build a broader vision that will make an impact on the whole planet.

You can have it all, but "all" needs to come from your joyful core. Along my journey, the only thing holding me back from joy was myself. Now I've stepped aside to open the floodgates to a big life. Will you?

Lorraine Francis has committed to environmentally responsible design for the past twenty years. During her tenure as an associate at Gensler, one of the world's leading architecture and interior design firms, she led many large-scale airport terminal projects, including Austin and Miami, and received the shared honor of the AIA Award of Merit for her San Diego Terminal 2 Expansion. In 1997, Lorraine founded Cadiz Design Studio. As an LEED accredited professional for Leadership in Energy and Environmental Design, Lorraine has a dedicated following of many respected clients in a multitude of sectors. Notable projects include the Starwood's Phoenician Resort, Sheraton Kauai, the Givenchy Spa in Palm Springs, and renovations for Warner Brothers and Goldman Sachs. She recently launched a few sister companies: CADIZ Collaboration, focused on sustainability consulting for businesses and homes; CADIZ Construction; and CADIZ Residential, both focused on sustainable residential renovations and commercial buildings. She has also launched a non-profit, Shades of Green Foundation, which teaches the principles of sustainability, making it achievable for all. Connect with Lorraine at www.beingLORRAINE.com.

Joy Long
There Will Always Be Dragons!

We all have dragons. Some plague and terrify us, while others are here to help guide us on our journey. Often they play both parts in our healing. What are your dragons? Sexual abuse? Addiction? A physical, mental or learning disability? Financial issues? A problematic job? Transformational work can connect each of us with the power and discernment we need in order to know whether the moment calls for us to battle, walk away from or integrate each dragon.

Born with everything I need, I am a duality—the Dragon Slayer and the Wisdom Keeper. These roles were not learned; they are innate and automatic, permeating every breath I take. They are light and dark, positive and negative. My journey—all of our journeys—is about learning to balance these seemingly disparate parts of self and using their profound wisdom for growth.

Before my adoption at age five, when I was about three and fighting to survive parental abandonment and sexual abuse by my "trusted" caretakers, the Wisdom Keeper in me emerged as a persona able to disassociate herself from what was happening to my body. She rose above, looked down, observed, gathered useful information and analyzed it to strategize the behavior that would keep me alive and as safe as I could possibly be, given the circumstances. I clearly remember deliberately offering myself to one of the abusers in place of another child, stepping in front of her and declaring: "You don't want her. Take me instead."

At that moment, the Dragon Slayer manifested as the part of me that fought the dragons of brutality and injustice by sacrificing myself to save others. A life pattern was set in place.

My whole life, I was very conscious of my armor and swords, of protection and fighting at every step. My weapons were my intelligence, my compassion, my communications skills, at times even my sexuality. These were the ways that I proved myself, and

> *My journey—all of our journeys—is about learning to balance these seemingly disparate parts of self and using their profound wisdom for growth.*

they had to be honed to the sharpest edge. With enough information, I'd be prepared for any scenario that might arise and was therefore protected. People would have to like me, respect me, see me as worthy—even love me—because I had an answer for everything. If I could fix or improve any situation, who could possibly reject me?

It seems odd to me now that as a young person, I was completely unaware of these two parts of my persona as coping mechanisms. So I certainly did not have names for them. I merely felt, acted and reacted—mostly reacted—in my heightened state of needed protection.

The Wisdom Keeper and Dragon Slayer worked together beautifully to allow my survival into adulthood. With their help, I fended off many a dragon.

Trouble was, I couldn't tell the difference between the dragons who breathed fire and those who were harmless when you got to know them, like Puff. My Dragon Slayer's armor was impenetrable, polished to a high gloss; but it was also heavy, like kryptonite. It was untouchable; and it weighed me down, keeping me from being free and flexible. I could not trust anyone, could not let in love. I thought I trusted myself, but the truth was I didn't. And I always had to do more, more, more to be good enough. I thought that if I just followed all of the "shoulds" and "ought-tos," I could slay all of the dragons and live happily ever after.

I did not realize I was living out of fear: of others hurting me, of being abandoned because I was not good enough, of being too good and not being able to sustain it. My anger, resentment and fear were internal weapons I handed my dragons to use against me—this put much of my power in the hands of others. Being in fight mode all of the time wore me out. I never filled myself up, so I was empty.

My accepting, friendly, open exterior showed the person I wanted to be, but was too afraid to truly become. I wish I had understood then that living from a place of fear was giving my power to the real *and* perceived dragons in my life.

The secret is: There will always be dragons. You can only control how you prepare for and respond to them. Many aren't dragons at all, but beings in dragon costume, taking on the world the only way

> *The secret is: There will always be dragons. You can only control how you prepare for and respond to them. Many aren't dragons at all, but beings in dragon costume, taking on the world the only way they know how.*

they know how. Such discernment comes not through denying our innate protectors, but by being aware of them and learning to let them help us in higher ways.

We all need coping mechanisms, every day! You don't have to divest yourself of them. When I first identified my Dragon Slayer and Wisdom Keeper, I saw them only as the disassociator and the blind fighter—a disturbing duality. I thought, *I shouldn't need them anymore.*

It was the "shoulds" and "ought-tos" I was struggling with. In ways, I was my own worst dragon! Transformational work showed me that my dual personas are actually gifts that I have to continually work to balance.

Once I realized that the Dragon Slayer and Wisdom Keeper were not just coping mechanisms, but part of my authentic self, the weight of the world was lifted from my shoulders. Full of adrenalin from being in constant fight mode, I had been holding my breath

> *The Dragon Slayer who awakens to the knowledge that the world is not as it seems is enlightened, empowered. This is the difference between false and true power.*

my whole life. Now I could breathe, and center into a core place— the positive, truly powerful aspect of the Wisdom Keeper. I realized that though the events that shaped me were painful, being a Dragon Slayer was something I had earned, and I could wear her new, permeable armor proudly.

It would be very easy for the Dragon Slayer to let fear and anger rule. But the Wisdom Keeper is like Merlin, the all-knowing seer, the mentor, a calm inner core that teaches the Dragon Slayer how to choose. She is the tether to reality who, if we listen to her, gives us all the information we need to know: Which dragons do we have to fight? Which do we tame? Which can we simply walk away from? The Wisdom Keeper gathers information and formulates battle plans: Which things do I need, and which do I not? Which pieces are making the castle crumble, and which fortify it?

The Dragon Slayer who awakens to the knowledge that the world is not as it seems is enlightened, empowered. This is the difference between false and true power.

The false bravado of a Dragon Slayer attaches to the idea that *I can be strong, because I have all these weapons*—versus recognizing and settling into true inner power. Having true inner power means knowing you don't always have to fight. Find not just that piece within that says *I can stand up*, but also the Wisdom Keeper who considers how you can do it in a centered way so it is more powerful, and not discounted. Love and compassion are the secret weapons of the Dragon Slayer standing in her true power.

Women especially need to cultivate the sense that we have the right to be protected, and the right to stand up and fight when need be. Despite some progress, ours is still not a society that encourages women to find their inner strength. We are still expected and taught to be subservient; to accept less and take it as a matter of course; to listen to that loud "other voice" that tells us we have to perform or change who we are to please others. And often when women do stand up against injustice, they are disparaged with comments about their emotions or hormones. "Oh, she's just having a hissy fit."

> *Your inner self, your core spirit,*
> *is your best armor and most effective*
> *weapon. Trust yourself. Remember, you were*
> *born with everything you need.*

Sometimes we need those weapons, just as we all need coping mechanisms. Discerning which to use when, instead of automatically drawing the sword, is the Wisdom Keeper balanced with the Dragon Slayer into one enlightened, empowered being—lift up the visor of the Dragon Slayer's helmet and you will be shown the Wisdom Keeper's face. They are not two separate parts, but balanced forces (some days better than others) on a quest to right the injustices we see outside ourselves, *and* those we perpetrate *against* ourselves.

Fortify your castle. Your evolution requires that you strengthen your foundation by eating well, moving your body, sleeping and rejuvenating. All these will help you feel better and think more clearly. And breathe! Breath is the center support of your castle. Seek out and recognize your sources of support, the people and things that make you happy. Surround yourself with them. They make your foundation stronger.

Give yourself permission—to be right sometimes and wrong sometimes, to be up sometimes and down other times, to laugh, to love, to just be. Every time you kick yourself around, it damages your foundation.

Assess your dragons. Rid yourself of assumptions—not every obstacle is a fire-breathing dragon. And consider the possibility that a dragon might have been sent to fight beside you, not against you. With every dragon you encounter, ask yourself: Is this an internal dragon or an external dragon? Is this real or perceived? Is this a dragon I have to take on? Is this a dragon that I must slay, or might I tame it instead? If I must slay this dragon, what weapons and strategies will work most efficiently so that the battle ends as quickly as possible? Are there ways to actually turn my relationship with this dragon into a win-win situation?

Your inner self, your core spirit, is your best armor and most effective weapon. Trust yourself. Remember, you were born with everything you need. Let go of what no longer serves your soul purpose!

On the path I'm walking now, the Dragon Slayer and the Wisdom Keeper move hand-in-hand. Together, they fortify the castle, keep the armor polished, and maintain a full arsenal of love and compassion. They need each other—I need them—in order for me to fulfill my own soul's purpose of bringing people to their power.

Let your armor be intact but permeable, so you can deflect negativity and let in the positive. Allow for a different way of thinking, and your Dragon Slayer and Wisdom Keeper will operate from your true inner power, your authentic self. That is the self so needed by the world, to fight large and small injustices.

A single life always makes a difference. Your individual light, and everyone else finding theirs, is the only way we can create a more loving, compassionate and therefore powerful world.

Joy Long is the owner and "Slayer in Chief" of DragonSlayer Strategies. Recently awarded recognition as Biltmore's 2010 Professional of the Year in Health Care Consulting, Joy has been instrumental in bringing together regulators, for-profit and non-profit organizations, community service entities and others as strategic partners for various projects. Joy's passion is helping individuals identify their dragons, fortify their castles and assess their armor and weapons. She is a certified Changeworks practitioner, has been adjunct faculty and guest lecturer at several colleges in the Indianapolis area and has acted as a trainer for many organizations. Joy has written articles published in journals, industry-specific publications and newspapers. She has also acted as a guest speaker and commentator on both radio and television. For more information on how you can find your inner Dragon Slayer for personal or for business transformation, visit www. DragonSlayerStrategies.com.

Debra Jean Smith

From Tomboy to Enchantress

Do you yearn to surrender to passion, to be swept away by a tidal wave of love like a romance novel heroine? You've read about passionate inner fire and watched it play out on the silver screen, but does that deep, sweeping force pulse through your own body? Does it nourish and feed your own soul? What if it *were* possible? What if the passion you yearn for could leap from the pages of romance novels and into your own life? What if it's already waiting within you, like a rosebud ready to burst into full bloom? YOU *can* awaken the sensuality and passion you have always dreamed about. I'm going to show you how.

When I opened myself to my own feminine sensual essence, I discovered a level of love, bliss and intimacy that opened my heart and thrilled me beyond all my dreams and imaginings. I felt more alive than I ever had, and my self-expressed, beautiful essence acted as a magnet, drawing an exponential flow of love and intimacy into my life. I realized that it didn't matter what I looked like or how old I was: it WAS possible. It gave me renewed hope that I could share with others.

As women, we are designed for pleasure. But since we usually get the opposite message, we learn to stifle our sexuality by denying our powerful, feminine sensual essence. That's why I'm here—to usher in a new generation of women owning our true sensual nature as open, free and fulfilled beings, surrendered to pleasure.

I discovered my own feminine sensual essence without a model to follow. My journey began in junior high school. I was a flat-chested tomboy who felt comfortable playing sports and hanging out with my brother and his buddies. The boys didn't see me as a "girl," because I could throw a ball as well as they did—I was "one of the guys." I respected, liked and related well to boys as well as to my girlfriends. And since I could relate well to both guys and girls, I became the go-between for all my friends and their relationships.

But then came high school. I had long blonde hair, blue eyes— all the stuff the Beach Boys were singing about at the time. I became popular overnight, met my very first boyfriend and fell in love. I didn't have a sense of my own self worth, my body or my

> YOU can *awaken the sensuality and passion you have always dreamed about. I'm going to show you how.*

sexuality, so I gave in to my boyfriend's repeated requests to "really love him." I didn't listen to my intuition, and naïvely gave away the most precious gift of my young body. Barely a few months later, I married him because I was pregnant.

Now that I was married, my less experienced friends considered me an expert on sex. But a whole year later, I was embarrassed to admit that I hadn't yet had an orgasm. I was more concerned with pleasing my husband, who had me convinced that there was something wrong with me, or my clitoris, or that I might not even have one. It didn't occur to me that he was young and didn't know what he was doing, either.

Distraught, I confided in my older brother-in-law, who gave me a copy of *Everything You Wanted to Know About Sex But Were Afraid to Ask*. Fortune smiled on me.

I soon learned how to self-pleasure—something my mom told me with that certain "look" when I was eight years old that girls shouldn't do. I grew up in a generation where we hardly talked about self-pleasure or sex at all. But once I started having orgasms, I was so excited I practically had to shout it from the rooftops. I wanted all my girlfriends to know about this. And I wanted to assist them in loving and exploring their bodies and experiencing pleasure and orgasms too. I realized then that I had the gift of being able to share about intimacy. I was comfortable, so it allowed others to feel comfortable confiding in me. So began my passion for passion.

I've discovered that one of our main blocks to feeling attractive and sensual is our body image. We're worried about our weight,

> *I've discovered that one of our main blocks to feeling attractive and sensual is our body image.*

our legs, our pooch tummies, our noses, our scars and so on; then, as we age and find brown spots and wrinkles, our self-image can get even further degraded. We project this poor self-image onto men and imagine they won't find us attractive. But let me tell you a truth: (most) men do not see our bodies the same way we do, despite all the billboards, magazine ads, films and television programs. They are far less critical, and rarely notice the flaws we are so concerned about—especially if they are our husbands and partners who love us.

My male clients and friends all tell me that their best intimate sexual experiences have been with women who did *not* have perfect bodies and were not the most attractive partners. Their best experiences were with women who were enthusiastic, confident and passionate: women who were accepting of their bodies, didn't worry and were excited to be with them and enjoy pleasure. When men are free to please their women, they get to express their masculine energy without fear. It is very affirming and a personal triumph for a man to give pleasure and assist a woman with having an orgasm. Did you notice that I said "assist us in having orgasms?" We are never given orgasms. We *allow* ourselves to experience orgasms.

Let me tell you about Joan, a forty-two year-old client of mine. Joan hadn't made love with her husband in almost two years because she had gained weight during peri-menopause and didn't feel sexy or desirable anymore. The first thing I asked her to do was to reconnect to her own body, her own sensuality. I had her explore, identify and articulate what was actually most pleasurable for her so that she could share that with her husband. I asked her to also start visualizing an intimate, romantic encounter with her husband.

Joan set up a date night that included everything that made her feel sensual and desirable. Attending to every detail, she bought a beautiful, sensual silk scarf to wear around her hips (an area where she felt unattractive); lit candles; arranged her favorite flowers in the bedroom; and put on soft music. She and her husband had the most romantic, heart-connecting evening they had shared in many years. It genuinely reignited their passion and love for each other. Her husband thought she was the most beautiful woman ever, because she was connected and wanting him. All it took was this shift!

Because Joan has given herself *permission to open without shame or guilt,* being her luscious sensual self, her real glow—her deep and soulful allure—is now her own. To help remove the guilt Joan was feeling, I had Joan say to herself, "It is my Divine birthright to create and enjoy pleasure. I can enjoy and relish every moment of my intimacy with my husband. I am designed for pleasure."

After years of guiding my friends and clients, I realized there was still a vulnerable place in my own heart that had yet to open. I had been single for five years, and was ready and yearning for an intimate connection. I set my intention to manifest a relationship, and began to visualize not so much what my man would look like, but how I would feel in my body and soul when I was with him. *Secure. Loved. Cherished. Protected.* I visualized this every day for several weeks. Then one day I met him at a friend's gathering. In a few short weeks, I realized that I was experiencing everything I had visualized.

I allowed myself to trust, surrender and open to my femininity as I had never done before. Doing that felt like a gigantic exhale. Letting go of my masculine energy was strangely liberating, and allowed him to meet me in the fullness of his masculinity and presence. I was left weeping in gratitude from the love, power and intimacy of our connection and lovemaking.

I had never *imagined* how spiritual and intimate a deep, sacred, sexual union could be until I opened to my sensual essence. When my relationship with him ended after seven glorious years,

> *I'm happy to say that once we have experienced our full feminine sexual potential, it's ours, always.*

I deeply questioned whether I could re-create and feel this with someone new. I realized, after taking some time for healing and re-adjustment, that I could, because the power and surrender was in me and not dependent on him. I'm happy to say that once we have experienced our full feminine sexual potential, it's ours, always.

You may be thinking, "That's all well and good for you, Debra, but what about me?" Or, "That's some kind of spiritual hoo-hah, but it's not for me." What really matters is that pleasure brings us back to who we really are and connects us to our partners. Did you know that we have over eight-thousand nerve endings in our clitoris alone? We were gifted with a clitoris and its sole purpose is *just for pleasure*. With or without a partner, you have the ability, through it, to reconnect to your body.

Because we were born for passion and designed for pleasure, anytime we settle for less than that, something in us diminishes and we are diminished by it.

Living passionately and sensuously is nourishment for the soul and spirit. Without it we just exist in the physical, emotional and mental realms—we don't really live. With passion, sensuousness and pleasure, the physical is heightened, the emotions improve and mental unrest is calmed. The body comes alive, health is instantly improved and spirits soar.

I know this to be a fact, and I choose to dedicate my life to experiencing it completely, and helping as many people as possible have the experience, too. For the more people that achieve this in their lives, the more peace, joy, satisfaction and fulfillment will come into the world.

You have permission. It's your birthright.

Debra Jean Smith, intimacy and sensuality guide, author and speaker, has been guiding her friends and clients for the past thirty years to enjoy deeper connection and more intimate pleasure. Debra has a unique ability and lightness that allows her clients to feel comfortable, safe and free from guilt. Her clients gain more passion and zest because their lives become empowered, enriched and nourished. The title of her new book is Permission to Enjoy: Secrets & Stories to Awaken Your Sensual Essence. *Visit www.TheSensualitySage.com.*

Rochelle Forrest

Shine Bright for the World

You are encoded with a divine spark, and your light—just like everyone else's—is uniquely necessary to the universe. You possess all the wisdom required for this Earth journey; everything you will ever need is within you right now. Your inner light is constant, always available and only waiting to be discovered. I'm here to tell you that you are *already* whole; you are a shining light! To know your wholeness will bring you into your true, divine being: your *holiness*.

If we neglect our hearts and our light, we can end up fragmented, compulsively seeking a feeling of wholeness through food, sex or other substitutes to try to escape pain.

Most of us hide from ourselves, our pain and our fears, and we tend to focus on what we *don't* want. But the potential for connection is always there. When we cultivate our connection with our true selves and with our source, we can set aside our harmful habits, stop hiding and begin to re-create our wholeness and live in our own holiness.

Your soul is here for a unique purpose. To plug back into your own light, journey within to find out what you really, really want. We may think we don't know what we want, but we really, really do! We're often busy working under other people's expectations at the cost of our own dreams and energy; but once we honor and claim our own space, then our next step, and the next… next… and next will unfold. Then we can each create a Life Plan, a template or blueprint for the future that we develop with a focus on what we want in the end. The beginning is where we are right now. The middle part, the journey into the light, is the really fun part!

How can you prepare to create a great plan for your life?

- Start by listing the critical moments in your past— the ones that made the biggest difference or left the deepest impressions. Note their impact. Do you see a pattern overall? If so, does it work for you?
- Reflect on the past. What unresolved issues still plague you? What would happen if you looked at them from a new and entirely different perspective? How might you re-frame them positively, so you could then move on to happiness?
- Now project into the future. When you think about where you want to be—in three months, a year, five years—what fears, worries or perceived limitations are holding you back in the present?
- After taking each of these baby steps, write down your observations. Then identify your dearest desires. You may think you'd like to have a lot of money, for example, but is that the real desire? Look deeper. Maybe the true desire is to be safe or to be loved.

You can learn and grow through this process. Sometimes you need to seek; at other times you need to allow ideas to find *you*, and say *yes* to them.

You can put full trust in your life's process: Know that each day you are growing and preparing for your higher purpose with the guidance of the divine.

Now you can go to the beginning of your new Life Plan to see where you are at this moment, and then lay out the steps you can take to get to where you want to be. Once you have truly defined your purpose and established a goal, you will get there, no matter what.

You can learn to live in the present moment. Allow yourself five minutes each day to just *be*. In this busy world, this is one of the most important things you can do to connect with your light. Take time to honor yourself and create a sacred space. Don't think, don't ask questions; just be still and listen for the answers, and they will come to you. (Isn't it interesting that the words *silent* and *listen* contain the same letters?)

Your spirit is limitless, but your body will create limitations if you don't take care of it. Let it be the magnificent vehicle that brings you to your heart's desires. Listen to what it is saying. As a nurse, I have seen many people resort to taking medications that

> *I'm here to tell you that you are already whole; you are a shining light! To know your wholeness will bring you into your true, divine being: your holiness.*

simply knock out symptoms instead of really paying attention to what their bodies are trying to tell them. Rather than ignoring the messages, focus on creating health. You can absolutely reframe your situation and find power in it. You can move past your limitations and take responsibility for what you've brought into being: mind, body and spirit.

My work is about helping people discover their core issues and their essence, what is fun and joyful for them, what makes them happy; but once upon a time I too had to totally re-frame my life. There I was, a young nurse wanting to heal others, but feeling tremendous personal pain (although I often felt very happy, too). I thought, *How can I serve well from a state of brokenness?* I had to get back to my core to see why I was repeating the same painful experiences. Then I had to re-frame my life story so that I could find my power.

I remembered sitting on the steps of our first family home. There I was, little Shelly, listening to my parents fight. My father was drunk, and my mother was crying and yelling, "You are so irresponsible!" Sitting there on the steps, that little girl I used to be felt invisible. And in that moment, little Shelly assumed full responsibility for making it all better. She learned to work hard at pleasing, pleasing, pleasing all the time. She learned to equate abuse with love. Later, she continually sacrificed herself to please others.

Years later, when I was in nursing school, some of my friends started calling me Rochelle instead of Shelly. I liked being called by my formal first name, which means *rock*.

As Rochelle, I re-framed my experience so I could re-member myself as shining among the living. I forgave my parents, because they had done the best they knew how. I spoke my heart and mind and let myself be bright. I re-framed my ideas about love and stopped giving myself away.

My adult self, Rochelle, has done a lot of work with inner child Shelly to reassure her that she is safe, worthy, loved and heard, to help her find peace and joy on the inside. That work has included

> *Once you have truly defined your purpose and established a goal, you will get there, no matter what.*

making my own Life Plan. I know I am following my plan, living in light and love, and serving joyfully so that others may bring their light into the world. And my light grows brighter every day.

Life has its seasons: time to prepare your soil, plant your seed, nurture yourself and allow yourself to blossom. Root your desires, and get grounded! Too many people uproot their desires before they have time to actually take root. If you don't have a Life Plan, you're living someone else's plan for you.

Ground your vision of what you want by doing something every day to affirm that you are following *your* plan. Write down a list of things that help bring you back to yourself, and each morning pick something from that list to do. Learn to quiet yourself to let your true voice through. Stop, breathe and believe. Lift up your palms to heaven. This will ground you and reconnect you with source, re-membering you to the whole.

Your journey is always to the self; all the answers are there. Know that, regardless of your age, there is a magnificent mission

> *You are singular, divine and necessary in the world. Honor your unique process.*

inside you, and the vitality of your life is directly proportionate to the vividness of your vision. Your calling whispers to you through your intuition, trying to pull you closer. When you really listen to that inner voice, it eventually becomes louder and more important than your critics.

When you follow your intuition and honor your calling, you will find inspiration, and your light will only grow. Whenever you have an intention, place your attention on it, and magic will happen. You are singular, divine and necessary in the world. Honor your unique process.

When my sons were little, they believed that my kisses had magical healing powers, so when they fell down, they ran inside for me to kiss their ouchies. Stereotypical boys, they always took big risks, and some days I dispensed a lot of kisses! One day I filled their hands with kisses and told them to put the kisses in their pockets. Then, if they fell down, they could reach in and take out a kiss to make the ouchie better.

They believed! I laughed so hard when I saw that, after falling down, they immediately reached into their pockets, took out kisses and placed them on their new ouchies. The power of their belief restored their bodies and spirits. They were healed, and off they went on new adventures.

I invite you to begin this wondrous journey to the heart of your true self. Arm yourself with faith and love for the little child inside you. Today I send *you* off with a handful of kisses to keep in your pocket. If ever you should trip and fall, simply reach in and get a kiss. Re-member, it has magical healing powers!

Shine so that others will shine, too!

Rochelle Forrest is a holistic health coach, professional speaker and author who works primarily with parents and entrepreneurs. Many are high achievers seeking to know their soul's purpose and to shine their light and make a difference in the world. The author of Re-Ignite Your Light *and* Core Reasons Why We Escape, *and founder of Create Health Naturally, Rochelle began her career as a registered nurse and went on to explore many different disciplines in pursuit of the universal principles of life and health. Her experience in healing has taught her that the mind, body and soul comprise the triad of health that springs from inner light. Learn more about Rochelle at www. CreateHealthNaturally.com.*

Zoya Bokhoor

Live It!

July 20, 2004, is a day that will never leave my mind. My son Roy
had spent the night at his friend's house and was still away that
morning when I went to a doctor's appointment. I was nervous;
they had found some abnormality in my breast tissue earlier, but
an exam showed that everything was okay. When I left the doctor's
office, I called Roy to give him the good news. He didn't answer, so
I left a message sharing it. "I feel our lives are taking a better turn,"
I said.

My husband had passed away from cancer less than two years
before, so the news about my health was particularly welcome.
During his dad's illness, Roy had become deeply depressed. But
he'd finally found a doctor he liked and trusted, was doing well on
medication and had even, after all he'd been through, managed to
finish law school in May. Everything was looking good: he'd found
a great job in New York City. We already had our plane tickets and
were excitedly scouting apartments.

All day I tried his phone—no answer. I started to worry, but
then told myself his phone battery must be out. Maybe he had no
way to recharge it. After work, I went to a gathering at my mother's
house. The rest of the evening I tried calling my son, and nothing.
At about eight p.m., I had a very uneasy feeling. I ignored it, but
then my cell phone rang. Thinking it was my son, I went outside

to pick up the call. I heard a stranger's voice, saying he was calling from the coroner's office. The voice told me that my son's friend had found Roy's body that morning; he had gone to sleep and never woken up.

"What?" I couldn't understand what the man was saying. "What's going on? Is my son sick? What's happening?"

"I'm surprised you haven't been contacted by the police yet," he replied.

I started screaming and couldn't stop. Everyone poured out of the house. They tried to pick me up off the pavement, but I couldn't move. I didn't know how to handle the pain. I wanted to disappear, somehow, and be with my son. How was I expected to keep on living? How was my family supposed to go through this? Everything was running through my head at a high speed—nothing made sense any more. My only son, gone?

I don't know if I slept that night, and the next day was a blur. But the next night was a magical one. I was sitting in a small heap outside my mom's house, which looks over the San Fernando Valley. At one point, when I looked up, the moon hung high over the mountains, bright in the distance. But when my ten year-old nephew came out not long after to point it out to everyone, it had already moved much further down and was large and red. I noticed it right away. *Wow*, I thought. *How did that happen?*

Then my nephew said, "I got a message from Roy. He is with his dad now. He's happy. And he wants you to use the second chance you've been given to live your best life, facing all your challenges." He said that Roy knew there would be hurdles to come, but he would always be with me, urging me to go on. He said I was meant to be happy, and that he and his father loved me. And he had great things yet to accomplish, in his new life. When the message was complete, my nephew said, "The moon is going to set." And we all watched, awed, as it went down behind the mountains. Then some great wave washed over us and the collective mood changed from sad and somber to joyful and hopeful. We all hugged each other happily, amazed at the transformation.

In the days that followed, Roy returned with more messages through my nephew; through my sister, who woke up one morning with a beautiful poem in her mind about him; and through my mother, who, distraught, called his name one night and distinctly, physically felt his presence. We all did.

This series of miracles showed me that there is life after death—my son had done everything he could to let us know that. And it showed me that I had a mission. Roy had a reason for telling me to stay. One day, driving down Ventura Boulevard, I saw the pain

> *It does no honor to our loved ones to live in misery. We are here to love each other and feel joy.*

I felt inside my heart on a homeless woman's face and thought, *No one should have to live that way.* I decided to help the homeless and opened a nonprofit organization by the name of Roy's Love Foundation, which is still active.

Roy's reason went deeper. A healer suggested I read a book written by a mother who lost her son in World War I and communicated with him after his death. He told her he was in an amazing place where he felt very happy. But he walked amongst many, especially children, who were in great pain because the loved ones they'd left behind suffered so much. I felt her message, deeply. It aligned with what Roy had told me: *Live your life and be happy.* I knew I was meant to say to people like myself: If you hold on to your anguish, it could be hurting your loved ones. That may sound crazy, but we just don't know. Why take the chance? It does no honor to our loved ones to live in misery. We are here to love each other and feel joy.

Even knowing that all of this was true, and that Roy was in a good place, I found life hard. The nights were horrible. I couldn't sleep for the intensity of my grief—it spiked in the night like illness, or fever. I felt guilty for having worked so much when he was little, and after his father's death; he had come home to an empty house too often. One night I was so distraught I could feel I was hurting him. And I said, "That's it. I'm going to stop."

I started seeing a psychologist. I realized I needed to do things that filled me up and made me feel alive. I decided to pursue art. I rediscovered my love for painting, and it has been so healing. I also took seminars with Landmark Education that helped me realize I had a choice, especially during the times I thought my heart would stop from sorrow. I had a choice between life and death. And my son helped me not only to choose life, but a life of freedom, generosity and love.

My son was my jewel; he had a presence like no one else. He used to say he thought he was an old soul. Roy was my teacher, all through his childhood; G-d was too generous with me to give me the honor of being his mom, even if it was only for twenty-four

> *If we let it, grief brings us back to our center. We're not here forever: What is the mark we want to leave?*

years. I can't talk about him enough, and whatever I say will not do him justice. I feel close to him still—I talk to him every day. His graduation picture from law school is on my desk. Sometimes I hug his photo.

I never found out the exact cause of Roy's death; there might have been some drinking involved, and alcohol and anti-depressants are a dangerous mix. But to me, the cause is immaterial. One of the biggest hurdles I had to overcome was my belief that what happened should not have, that it is wrong for children to die before their parents. But this is a rule we created. No one is here for eternity. We're here to do what we signed up to do and leave. I now believe that Roy did what he was meant to do in this life. When he was finished, when it was his time, he moved on to important and beautiful work elsewhere.

If I did not feel sure of that, if I had not received his messages, I don't think I would have the life I do right now. Roy is still teaching me. He has helped me so much, by being here and showing me that I can always choose what I create. I can create a positive, loving reality and help others heal; or I can stay stuck in my grief and suffering and miss out on living a real, full, vibrant life.

Grief is a wonderful teacher. It shows you how to change your point of view and really notice what's important in life. We are so used to running after material satisfaction that we are not being aware of what's really, really vital to us all—generously sharing the

> *The way you live your life affects*
> *everyone around you. We're all connected.*
> *Today is another day: Honor your loved one*
> *by bringing your whole self to the world,*
> *free to love, give and receive.*

love we have for each other, and discovering why we are here. Instead of suffering over your loss, live for your highest self in positivity, and build on that, rather than on a crumbling foundation of dug-in sorrow. Be present to create something beautiful and amazing and to make a difference in others' lives. That will do great honor to the memory of those you have lost. If we let it, grief brings us back to our center. We're not here forever: What is the mark we want to leave?

Before Roy's death, I spent a lot of time *wanting:* a happier family, a better job. I wasn't *living* my life; I was reacting. Now, with all the grief and loss, I can really feel happiness. It has come to me through getting in touch with my spirituality, doing a lot of soul-searching and *wanting* to find it. Happiness like this used to be a wish for someday. Being present to the beauty and love in the world has brought it home. I have remarried, to the love of my life. I have found my purpose in encouraging others who have felt great loss.

You have so much to build, out of your love. And you can only live your own life—you cannot complete anyone else's story. Start learning about yourself. Create an environment where you can move forward positively, as I did when I found art and Landmark classes. Research your options; see what groups are available. Try different avenues and see what feeds you. If you have the want, you will find the way. Don't give up, no matter what. If you have to take a day or two to be sad and cry, do. But on the third day, get up again and be loving and nurturing to yourself—it doesn't help anyone or change anything if you don't.

Talmud says, if you save a life you have saved the world. That includes your own. When you create your own life and live it with gratitude, passion and abundance, you hold your loved one's memories high and cherish them as if they were still with you. They just might be, but we don't know it.

We don't know where we come from; we don't know where we will go. The only thing we know is what we know, and that is here. The way you live your life affects everyone around you. We're all connected. Today is another day: Honor your loved one by bringing your whole self to the world, free to love, give and receive.

I have not had a direct message from Roy since the days just after his death, but if I did, I would hope he would still say: *I'm very happy. I am where I'm supposed to be.* I think he would also tell me: *Mom, I love you, and I'm very proud of you for what you've done so far. Keep going. Don't give up.*

Zoya Bokhoor provides administrative support and online marketing for entrepreneurs through her website, www.ZOfficeOnline.com. She has also created a web community for people who are grieving to come together and support each other, www.HealingWithCompassion.info; and is the founder of Roy's Love Foundation, www.RoysLoveFoundation. com. Connect with Zoya at www.ZoyaOnline.com.

Runa G. Bergmann

Women Can Change the World

M y love for nature in its various forms can be traced back to
my childhood. I was just a baby when my parents started
traveling with me, and, by the time I was five or six, camping
trips were the norm most summer weekends. We packed all our
camping gear on the roof rack of the old Willys Jeep my dad had
bought from the surplus equipment of the U.S. Army stationed in
Iceland after World War II. Import licenses for cars were rationed,
and only a few cars were available on the market, but my dad
always found a way to own one.

As we explored the back roads of Iceland, I learned the names
of mountains, valleys and waterfalls. My mother never tired of
telling us tales of elves and trolls, Viking-age sagas, and stories
of poets and visionaries who dreamed of Iceland's independence.
I learned of sacred places in nature that were to be honored and
respected, and so caring for the environment and loving the land
became a natural part of my upbringing.

My parents led by example, and always made sure to leave every
place in perfect condition; not only taking away our waste, but at
times also waste that others had left behind. No one talked about
environmental protection in those days. My family just lived it.

After graduation from college, I fell in love and became the
woman behind the man. Instead of pursuing further education, I

went to work in our fashion business, which grew over time into several fashion boutiques, a clothing-manufacturing company and record stores.

My husband and I spent a great deal of time every year pursuing outdoor activities such as angling, hunting and skiing. We were true soul mates and loved nature. Many of our happiest moments took place outdoors. I still remember staying awake through summer nights. It is truly magical. Iceland's twenty-four-hour daylight bonds you with nature in a mystical way. In the late eighties, I left our fashion business to open the first metaphysical bookstore in Iceland. This was the beginning of a new era, and

> *I still remember staying awake*
> *through summer nights. It is truly magical.*
> *Iceland's twenty-four-hour daylight bonds*
> *you with nature in a mystical way.*

my husband and I suddenly found ourselves at the forefront of the New Age movement in our country. Most of the self-help books were in English, so we started a publishing house in order to be able to offer them in Icelandic.

Along with books on personal development, I sold books on the environment, and was among the very few to celebrate Earth Day in Iceland. My husband and I sent suggestions for sustainable improvements to the city of Reykjavík in a competition that no one ever won, probably because the suggestions were too challenging. At home I separated waste, although the early-stage recycling station dumped it all in a landfill. I hosted a radio show encouraging people to protect and preserve the environment, spoke at public gatherings and wrote articles on the same subject.

In the early nineties, we became part-owners of a farm on Snaefellsnes Peninsula in West Iceland. The vision was to open a retreat, but none of the owners were committed to follow up on it. In 1994, we surprised everyone around us by deciding to do just that. We sold all our businesses and our home in Reykjavík to form—with a few friends who later joined us—the first sustainable community in Iceland. We created an environmental policy for the community, and adhered to it from the very beginning.

I no longer wore city shoes, as rubber boots were needed while I planted trees, ploughed land, planted potatoes and vegetables, painted the house inside and out and built furniture. I kept separating the waste, and drove it to what was then the only recycling station, one hundred and sixty miles away.

We were in the energy field of Snaefellsjokull Glacier at Hellnar, called by some psychics the "Heart Center of the Earth." The glacier was the first thing I saw when I opened my front door in the morning. It became "my glacier." Living in the energy field of the glacier challenged us to open our hearts and learn to love everything in a different way.

I studied shamanism with Native American teachers, developed my psychic abilities, became a certified yoga teacher and Reiki master and started leading my own self-empowerment workshops for women. As I empowered other women, I empowered myself—and transformed from the woman behind the man to the woman *beside* the man.

In between daily chores at the community, I put on my "city shoes," as I called them, and went to meetings and conferences. Some of them were in Iceland or on mainland Europe, while others were as far away as New Zealand. My purpose was always to speak on sustainable development of communities and tourism. At other times I just sat at my computer, wearing my Birkenstocks and writing articles on sustainable tourism for national and international magazines.

Our sustainable community didn't grow beyond the initial group that started it, but what did grow out of it was Hotel Hellnar, which became the first eco-certified tourism business in Iceland in 2002. I went back to school to study tourism at the University of Iceland. Our vision then was to see Iceland lead the way in sustainable tourism and become the first fully eco-certified country in the world.

At the turn of the twenty-first century, that vision was too big for most officials in Iceland. But the local governments on Snaefellsnes Peninsula were inspired by our vision, and one Minister was broad-minded enough to support a pilot project there. Green Globe trained my husband and me in the certification process, so we became two of a team of three that led the project. In 2008, all five municipalities on the Peninsula became the first in the Northern Hemisphere to be certified by Green Globe, whose name had by

> *We must dare to dream big. Only then do things that can really change the world start to happen.*

then changed to Earth Check. I wore high heels for the occasion and cried tears of joy. We must dare to dream big. Only then do things that can really change the world start to happen.

My husband didn't live to see that day. He passed away at our home in December of 2004. He had always said he wanted to die at the click of a finger, before me and at home. All three of his wishes were granted—but that meant I was suddenly left as a single woman. Having been part of a team for almost thirty-five years, I had a lot to learn about being alone, creating change alone and finding joy alone. Living at "the end of the world"—as I sometimes called the location of our hotel and home—with a partner who had been my best friend and co-worker, was isolating in many ways. After his death I was engulfed by our business and became even more isolated.

Yet I knew I needed to find a way out into the community again, and connect with more women. I knew in my heart that the next shift in environmental protection would come through them. Women have a power so many of them are neither aware of nor willing to exercise responsibly. What I am referring to is women's *power of purchase*. Women make more than eighty percent of all consumer decisions, and through that power they decide what appears on stores' shelves and racks and what does not. Many of them are already doing their share for the environment, but more are needed to shift global warming.

I have watched global warming in action melt my glacier away. Only five years ago, scientists estimated it would take fifty years for the snowcap to disappear completely; but a year ago new data showed that it could be gone in thirty years. I have also watched the sea birds near my home die of hunger as their staple food, a small sardine, disappeared when the ocean warmed. These are only two of many signs indicating that we are headed in the wrong direction and need to change course.

Through all the years I have been working on environmental protection, the words of my Native American teacher and grandmother, Twylah Nitsch, have kept ringing in my ears. She said at one of her teaching lodges: "the one thing we could not live without is air." Yet we are living in a world where the air is steadily becoming more and more polluted, leading to respiratory diseases

> *We can live without food and water for several days, but only for a few moments without air. Yet we keep polluting this life-giving substance—to a point where it poisons our bodies.*

and cancer. Our focus needs to be on cleaning the Earth's air, as that will also reduce global warming. Women can play a key role in this change, and leave a great legacy for future generations. We can live without food and water for several days, but only for a few moments without air. Yet we keep polluting this life-giving substance—to a point where it poisons our bodies.

Caring for the environment has been dressed in hippie clothes and sandals for too long. It needs to be moved to a new level and made fashionable, fun and a bit sexy—women can be all those things and still care for the environment. It is, after all, OUR environment. I've made it my mission to be a spokesperson for it, because that's just who I am. Not all women need to take it to the same level I do. They can contribute in smaller ways, as many small things lead to big results.

So whether you prefer green heels, flip-flops, slippers, boots or snowshoes (I've worn them all) you can easily contribute to change. Here are three easy tips: Carry a reusable shopping bag in your purse for items you buy. Separate your waste; recycle and reuse as much as possible. Buy carbon offset for your car—it costs so little and can mean so much when it comes to cleaning the Earth's air.

My message to all women is merely this: Let's not wait for a dramatic disaster situation before we make a move to change the world. Let's make the move now, while we can still turn things around. Let's head into a greener, safer future for all of us, a future created by women through their tremendous power of purchase.

Runa Gudrun Bergmann is a visionary entrepreneur who has devoted her life to creating a greener and more eco-friendly world. She owns international businesses, and devotes her time to writing, public speaking and creating new ways to inspire women to take the lead and change the world. She has recently launched a project called Green Heels, which makes caring for the environment fashionable, fun and sexy.

Runa has received numerous awards for her contribution to environmental protection, including 2004 Tourism Entrepreneur of the Year. She has appeared in documentaries and television programs in the United States, Canada, Denmark, France, England and, most recently, Germany, where she was featured in the Faces of Europe *series. Runa has written many articles for national and international magazines, and eleven books in Icelandic. Two of her books have been translated and published in the United States, Austria and Norway. Her most recent book,* Women Can Change the World, *will be published in Germany in 2011. Connect with Runa at www.GreenHeels.com.*

Carrie Woodburn

The Alchemy of the Heart

Transformation. To live life fully engaged is, by definition, to embrace transformation. Like the chrysalis becoming the butterfly, we are meant to progress through the tension of journeying deep into the human experience in order to discover the richness of our spirit.

I used to believe that my spiritual journey somehow meant transcending the drama and emotion of the human experience. I give thanks that I've discovered the blessings in embracing, observing and resting in my humanity from a place of compassion and discernment. I've learned to slow down so that I can hear and commune with the longing of my feminine heart. This life is a journey. And it is in the journey that our stories reveal to us who we really are.

I believe every woman has a story, unique as the strands of her own DNA. And every one of our stories contributes to the collective story, the human story.

My story is of a woman whose heart had been broken. Broken down, broken up and—what a blessing—broken open. My journey has been one of liberation and faith: a journey encompassing a mother, a daughter and a lineage. Mine—yours—in the collective they are not exclusive. And it is through our stories that we heal the hearts of women.

Recently, following the completion of my marriage of twenty years, the subsequent trauma of losing connection with my teenage daughter and the breaking up of all constructs I had for who I thought I was, I stumbled upon a place of unbearable suffering and shame. I stood at the edge of a very dark place—and surfaced into grace. And through it, the alchemy of my heart held space for my essence and beauty to emerge from the heat of transformation.

As a child, I was conditioned to be who I needed to be for others. So much so that I had lost any faculty for standing for what was best for me. Although I knew with every fiber of my being that I needed to change, I found it almost impossible to do so in the face of guilt and shame for what it would mean for my loved ones. When I finally knew that the pain of resisting change would

> *The only way to integrate, to become*
> *a woman who does not abandon herself,*
> *is to embrace all aspects of self.*

ultimately consume me, I risked the "unknown" and began to walk in honor of myself, willing to trust that my true path would lead to a well of wonderment and ultimately teach my children by example that they too would be safe honoring their truth.

It took time, and I would like to have handled some things differently. I lost my daughter for a while, but in the process I believe I gave her the gift of breaking the accommodating, self-abandoning traits the women in our family have carried for generations. I chose not to pay this forward in the lineage. I wanted better for her, for my grandchildren and for me. In the wake of change, I discovered myself. I have discovered a well of creativity within me, an artist I didn't even know who lived and breathed within me. I am painting, cooking, dancing, sharing and loving in ways I'd never allowed before. I am *in* love.

What I am describing is transformation. One that began with the awareness of the choice to become liberated from fear. Through letting go the bonds of fear and beliefs that simply are not so, I am blessed with an experience of falling over a waterfall in love with myself! Being liberated from fear does not mean absence of fear. It is simply acknowledging the fear, and not being stopped by it. We don't need to distract ourselves with worry about getting rid of fear or dark emotions. The work is in refusing them any significant meaning. They simply are. But that does not mean they have power of governance over you.

> I believe there is a massive awakening of the feminine occurring within the heart of all humanity. And as we listen, we begin to heal ourselves and heal our ancestral lineage both back-ward and forward in time.

The only way to integrate, to become a woman who does not abandon herself, is to embrace all aspects of self. To intimately know your fear, shame, guilt or whatever fragments you is to know its very flavor. Then, when that resonance is present for you in a room, a conversation or a relationship dynamic, you are aware of it. It no longer runs the show. You have a choice to either engage with it or simply observe it without it distracting you from your divine sacred truth. Being willing to really look at *myself* in the mirror to see, trust and honor the truth which courses through me, regardless of circumstance, well, that feels like Love.

I believe there is a massive awakening of the feminine occurring within the heart of all humanity. And as we listen, we begin to *heal ourselves* and heal our ancestral lineage both backward and forward in time. It's interesting, isn't it, that women love others so effortlessly—and yet the natural act of loving self is elusive for most of us? In a deep-rooted patriarchal society, women's voices are but a whisper. The influence of our lineage of generations groomed to serve, occupy secondary roles and not make demands on others is so potent, it is as if it is encoded in our very DNA. But as we learn to listen to the whispering of our feminine hearts, we can hear the voice of our divinity calling us forth to liberation.

For centuries women have embodied the system for creation, for attuning to great wisdom. Women are healers. And in the process of liberating ourselves from constructs and beliefs that hold us in a distorted conversation of "less than," "not good enough," self-sacrifice, guilt and shame, we come to a purity within that actually pulses with the heartbeat of the call of Spirit. In responding to the pull of our heart and spirit we pioneer new terrain for all to heal, and so heal and liberate the planet.

> *In responding to the pull of our heart and spirit we pioneer new terrain for all to heal, and so heal and liberate the planet.*

How we do this is simple, really. The act of listening to what our bodies and feelings are pointing us toward opens an access point in us for communing with our heart and spirit. With our eyes open to "see" our truth and respond in kind, we begin the journey of forgiveness and self-love, finding a soft resting place in the comfort of knowing we are connected in oneness. Honoring the individual call of our heart leads us to experience the healing creative juices alive in the abundance of connection to Earth, Spirit and all that is.

Women are connected by an invisible red thread. We are part of a collective sisterhood, each of us a mother or a daughter. All of us creators. And our stories, the stories of women—they heal. Through our love, our sorrow, laughter and pain, we shed sweet tears of honesty and enrichment. Our tears feed the soil of this great Earth and allow us to walk in the example of the Mother, as we die to the old to sprout from the new, over and over again, cultivating the Garden of the Sacred Feminine within us. We have a choice in how we walk this journey of life. Ask yourself: "How am I going to walk? Am I going to walk in apology, or am I going to walk in honor?"

I believe we are giving birth to a new paradigm that encourages us to rest in the wondrous ways of women such that we honor ourselves and the sisterhood of women, and to open for the men in our lives so they can experience a shift in their own orientation as men. How can they truly see and experience us until we've rested in the lusciousness of connection within ourselves? The same goes for all of our loved ones. How can they possibly savor the sweet nectar of our pure essence if we are scarcely sipping of it ourselves? What does your life look like with you fully embodying your feminine authority, sovereignty, beauty and grace? Can you imagine the richness of creation's desire coursing through you? Oh, the expansion!

> *The sacred feminine lives in all beings and is not exclusive to women. We all embody both masculine and feminine energy, and the collective of humanity knowing reverence for the feminine spirit will bring us back to the ways of honoring and healing the planet.*

The health and wellbeing of the tribe—whether it be in the broader context of humanity or a more regional context of community or family—depends on the health and wellbeing of women. It is women who are responding to our Mother Earth's call to heal from the deepest depths of the womb. When we respond to the impulse of our womb-space, our sacred vessel, we activate the medicine woman within and learn to walk in honor of ourselves and all that is.

It is no wonder we have gone into a collective slumber. In the Middle Ages, over nine million women were burned for practicing rituals of the Goddess. Our cellular memory knows something of this infliction of trauma, pain and suffering. But isn't it time we awaken? The impulse we are collectively experiencing as women to evolve and heal *is* the Sacred Feminine.

She exists in our veins. Breathes within our breath. And she is asking us to heal our feminine hearts. She is asking us to remember who we are. She knows we are here to heal the lineage of women. She understands that from the pains of labor are birthed the glory of God and Goddess. She asks if we are willing to dive into the depths and richness of our waters—both clear and murky—with love and compassion. She asks if we are willing to leave nothing unseen in the shadows of the darkness, nor unexpressed in the realms of our truth. And she knows that in the recognition of our own hearts, we are blessed to dwell in the place of grace.

The sacred feminine lives in all beings and is not exclusive to women. We all embody both masculine and feminine energy, and the collective of humanity knowing reverence for the feminine spirit will bring us back to the ways of honoring and healing the planet.

From the ashes rises the Phoenix. And, like alchemy turning base metal to gold, our hearts naturally transmute our pain to love. I call this the "Alchemy of the Heart." And basking now in the light of the gold that is coming forth in creation, out of the soot of *my* shame, feels like glory. It is extraordinary. I feel deeply blessed to rest in feeling the earth under my feet, and the steady beat of my feminine heart.

My prayer is that the expression of my heart touches others in a way that brings hope. Restoration. And a gentle reminder of faith. And as the chalice of my sacred heart fills and floweth over, I trust it to touch others in recognition of their own heart. Blessed Be.

Carrie Woodburn is a Certified Energy Health Practitioner (CEHP) and Certified Pranic Energy Healer. Alchemy of the Heart evolved out of Carrie's commitment to effect positive change in her community and the world. Her practice of healing and integration supports others to heal, awaken and realize freedom from addictions, fear-based limitations, limiting belief systems, physical pain and emotional or spiritual turmoil. Clients experience deep real life transformation, increased clarity, serenity and joy. Her workshop, "Cultivating the Sacred Feminine," creates a powerful foundation for participants to step forth into the expansion and intimacy of their own feminine hearts. Carrie facilitates retreats and workshops worldwide. Her programs awaken, inspire and empower people to enjoy a richer experience of their own brilliance and success both personally and professionally. Connect with Carrie at www.AlchemyOfTheHeart.net

Nancy Sommers

A Strong Finish

At four in the morning, hundreds of us are gathering on the bank of the Russian River for the Vineman Half Ironman Triathlon. Athletes of varying ages and skill levels crowd the bike stations and the river, putting on swim caps and readying their bikes for quick retrieval after the opening swim. Some athletes have set goals to improve their time from a past race, some are trying to win their age group, and some, like me, have set a goal just to finish strong.

Groups are already being launched—I hear the cracks of the starting gun in the early morning fog. The air buzzes with an intense vibration of excitement, adrenaline running straight through the athletes. I can feel the flow of energy connecting each of us.

The fog softens the bright colors of the age-correlated swim caps, and makes nearby voices sound as if they're coming from far away.

As I stand on the riverbank in my wetsuit, waiting to dive in for the 1.2-mile swim, the first phase of the race, I feel the anticipation manifesting in my body. I'm nervous, but I know that months of training have prepared me well. I think about my Tri Club friends already in the water, but it's impossible to spot a familiar face through whitewater splashes and bobbing caps. I hear the spectators' cheers and know my support team is out there, rooting me on. The Tri Club presence is strong.

I pick a spot to stand with my age group. I already feel pride swelling within me, knowing that when the swim ends and I depart the water, I will be on my way to fulfilling a major life goal. Positive affirmations surge through me as I look out at the sea of caps and whitewater, and at the women in my age group. *How amazing they look—they're lean and in great shape. So many of them have done this race or another race before. Now I stand ready to do my very first triathlon—I know this day is going to change my life!*

My thoughts shift to the great coaching I've received, the solid training to race and *finish*. Yes, that's my goal for the day, to *finish and finish strong*. I've been marathoning for years and training triathlon for months; I'm prepared and well coached. In this

> Some athletes have set goals to improve their time from a past race, some are trying to win their age group, and some, like me, have set a goal just to finish strong.

moment, the idea is to stay focused and remember: "The race is not won on the swim," which is my weakest event. I've overcome so much to arrive at this moment. I step into the water, hear the crack of the starting gun and suddenly, my self-confidence surges strongly. I'm on my way!

I realized my gift of speed as a child, when my family drove from Washington state to California every summer. Every year my cousin, a boy my same age, insisted on racing me the second I stepped out of the car. Year after year we grew and changed, but he was always eager for a competition, wanting to see if he could finally beat me.

As the years passed, memories of my childhood as a happy young athlete faded, overshadowed by family adversity. A series of traumatic events took away the joy and self-confidence I had once felt, and the desire to develop my God-given athletic talents. Instead, as a coping mechanism, I learned avoidance and mastered "acting as if." Eventually I became a Hollywood housewife, living a life that was perfect by all outward appearances. I had found a way to survive and was just going through the motions, accepting all the limitations I put on myself over my lifetime.

Throughout my growing years, I wore a layer of extra weight as an unconscious attempt to protect myself, and I had gone through a lifetime of yo-yo dieting. Finally, when I was in my late thirties, I started a program based on the book *Body for Life*. Not

> *As my physical abilities increased, my mind expanded to believe in my ability to accomplish anything.*

only did it change my body, it shifted my perspective on my whole self. Through journaling and following the twelve-week program, I developed new and life-changing habits. For the first time, I understood that I had to love myself; I had to value and care for myself from the inside. I was able to grow and expand my mind to allow for this new change and self-respect.

As a result, my great passion for athletics was reawakened. I got fitter than I'd ever been in my life, became a certified pro trainer and started running marathons.

As time passed in my new mind and body, I realized that if I could achieve *this* success, and *this*, then the possibilities were endless! I came to realize the only limits I'd ever had came from self-limitations that began in childhood.

Working as a volunteer at the World Championship Ironman Triathlon in Kona, Hawaii, for several years, I was exposed to athletes of all levels; so it wasn't long before I began multi-sport training, which led to the big event—the triathlon. Multi-sport training allowed my body, mind and spirit to become a unified athletic force. I bought a bike and fell in love with cycling. I was shaping into a true triathlete, with the growing confidence necessary for competition and a strength and perseverance I had never known before. As my physical abilities increased, my mind expanded to believe in my ability to accomplish anything.

Now, at Vineman, in this surreal moment of living my truth through my passion, I gather my thoughts and look ahead down the river. I realize how well coached I am. *I have this! Time to focus. Head down, high elbow, breathe, use your arms, save your legs.* I keep my eye on the riverbank to stay on course both physically and mentally.

I feel real triumph as I finish the swim, my weakest link: *now it's behind me!* Until today, I'd never swum this distance, even in training! But never again will I doubt my ability to swim 1.2 miles.

> *Because of my strength and training, I am living my dream.*

One event down, two left to go. Elation and pride sweep through me as I peel out of my wetsuit and head straight uphill on my bike for the fifty-six-mile ride—my favorite event. I know that, on my bike, I can make up any time I lost in the swim.

My training pays off yet again as I ascend the infamously famous Chalk Hill, and I climb with ease and grin, realizing how prepared I am both mentally and physically, *I had this!* And I remind myself that *This is just another training day.*

Reverberating with excitement, I settle into feeling the fun and taking in the beauty of the surrounding wine country. Cameras snap, and I hear the voices of complete strangers cheering my name. I feel confident, fast and strong—I'm actually one of the "athletes" being cheered on! Because of my strength and training, I am living my dream.

As I approach the finish of the cycling portion, I am overwhelmed by the number of people who come out to support us. I jump off my bike, change shoes, turn my race number from my back to my front and take off for the run. The fog burned off long ago, and now it's hot on the open streets, with few trees to offer shade. The weather and the elements are a huge part of any Ironman event; I know this, so I'm well prepared with the necessary nutrition and hydration.

At about mile ten, I have to walk a little, and coach myself with positive self-talk: *You can do this. You're almost there.* The sun feels merciless, but I keep the finish in my mind: the medal, the photos, the friends and family that will be there to rejoice with me. I recall the shouts of my name throughout the day from perfect strangers, people who believed in me and were inspired by me.

I think of the glory I'll feel just finishing. *My first triathlon, and I'm finishing a half Ironman!* I'm finishing the race sore and tired, with blisters and lost toenails, but I feel great. I hear my name yelled from the sidelines, and it gives me the final burst of joyous energy I need to ignore the pain and cross the finish line. I've done it!

We all have the power to change our thoughts and feelings by creating new habits and getting rid of old belief systems. You don't have to become an athlete to find your passion and live your dreams. Once you understand and believe that you have the power to transform your whole being—physically, mentally, emotionally and spiritually—you have connected the key elements to happiness and a life of fulfillment and joy. What happened in the past is in the past. Change your habits, and you will change your life.

We are all the creators of our lives. When we can recognize and accept that power, transformation through anything is possible. The life of your dreams becomes the life of your reality. It is within your reach, too!

Nancy Sommers is an author, speaker and entrepreneur, as well as a certified fitness professional and triathlete. She is currently working on her book, The Spirit of Riley. *She is also a contributing writer for* The Passion Test eMagazine. *Her goal is to one day do the full Ironman race in Kona, Hawaii, and use resulting media and sponsorships to benefit a non-profit she is developing to support women and children and their beloved pets in finding safe housing. Connect with Nancy at www.NancySommers.com.*

Laura Ellsworth

Say Yes to Success

Every woman on this planet has the ability to live in her full essence, her full beauty, grace and power. This includes having financial success!
—Kimber Lim

The backbone of our country is based on small business and innovative thinking from entrepreneurs. The way we do business has changed forever, and transformational thinking and the sharing of resources will rebuild the world economy and support the good that each of us can create. Looking back over thirty years of entrepreneurship, the only thing I wish I'd had in the early days is a network of trustworthy mentors, especially ones who could point me in the right direction when it came to resources, and help me to balance my life as a wife, mother *and* entrepreneur.

Ever since kindergarten, I've known what I wanted: motherhood, helping people, lots of creative expression and to be an entrepreneur.

Working on my art projects, and always believing in the possibility of any idea, has kept me afloat through challenging times. Anything I've learned, I've done well. When I was a teenager, macramé was a big trend. I created a large wall hanging, and it ended up winning first prize among all the high-school-age artists in Los Angeles county that year.

People loved my stuff, so I brought macramé pot hangers to a local flower shop at the mall and sold them. At age sixteen, I got my first seller's permit (the same number I operate under today). Having my own business was fun and inspiring!

But I didn't know how to build a business, and I never had a mentor to show me. So for a long time, I worked a low-paying, full-time job in a commercial art-supply store. After a year of training at art school, I learned the fine art of custom picture framing, and I made an arrangement with the store to do my framing after hours, in exchange for a percentage of sales. I worked every day from eight to five and did my framing at night from six to twelve.

News of my work spread among the right people, and the framing business grew enough to become full-time by word of mouth alone. I had a great list of clients, including Dr. Phil, NBC and Warner Brothers. Hanna Barbera was my favorite! I kept up with my own business education by reading and attending seminars. I have a son and daughter that I am very proud of. My husband and I worked hard to support our family, but I always hoped for business to be at a higher level.

When my daughter was five, I was watching cartoons with her when an infomercial came on that caught my attention. I bought a thirty-dollar program to "become prosperous from home" that got me on what appeared to be every mailing list on the planet.

That may sound awful, but in my case it was a blessing. Reading over all the materials I got in the mail amounted to an intensive course in marketing. I clearly saw what techniques worked and which did not. I developed a critical, analytical eye for business I'd never had before. I could tell at a glance which outfits were surely selling snake oil. Those companies that appeared credible, I researched. And in this way, I began vetting resources for myself that I would eventually put to great use.

Mostly, though, my focus was on the best life for my family. I had big dreams for my children, but I also wanted a larger model for my business. When my children left home, it was a bit of a shock. Not only did I miss them a lot, I realized I hadn't planned my life for me, or for what I would do when they were gone. I was at that point in mid-life when I asked myself, "Who am I? Am I living my best purpose?" I knew I wasn't living my full potential. I wanted to grow personally and as a businesswoman and I wanted to help people. I was passionate about business-building, art and wellness products. Over the years I had found amazing natural products that had turned my own health from seriously problematic to vibrant. I knew I needed to get Internet-savvy, and create a presence there.

> *What I was looking for were people with years of experience behind them, and what they had consistently been able to help create for others. Now those were the people I wanted to know about!*

I started going to women's groups and listened to what all the ladies were looking for and trying to evolve into. In many voices, I heard echoes of my own. And in many others, I heard potential for my own direction. One group offered free mentoring, and I took advantage of that wonderful resource I'd never had before to help guide the new unfolding that was happening in my life. It was time to say *yes* to success.

Until now, network marketing programs had, for the most part, failed me; they had lacked the training and support I needed. The presenter of one event I was invited to, a woman who billed herself as a "prominent speaker," showed up in my research as someone with enough charisma to attract crowds to her events, but little experience and knowledge to back herself up. She'd been doing it for less than a year. *10K a day for close access to her "expertise?"* I thought. *You're kidding!* Later, women I knew who had gone to her seminar described their disappointment and frustration. The road to success seemed littered with such dead ends. What I was looking for were people with years of experience behind them, and what they had consistently been able to help create for others. Now those were the people I wanted to know about!

When I market my art and wellness products, all the resources I draw from are linked to ones I've vetted thoroughly and with which I have already had positive experiences. It saves so much time to know quality people and companies with whom to affiliate! When I sell art prints, for example, I know the quality of the work and materials and the artist's or supplier's abilities for order fulfillment. Any wellness products I feature I have tried and have researched for longevity, reorder rate and sustainability. Every piece of the puzzle is solid.

If you don't have the right people to tell you what to do and how to do it, it's like jumping into the ocean and drowning. It's very common for women, especially those who have raised kids, to look

> *Your passion is within you: it just needs to be identified. Some people know what it is right away; for others it needs to be coaxed out. So look for mentors you can trust to boost your process.*

around at mid-life and say, "What now?" You have a passion and a purpose, and all is available to you if that passion is part of your balance, your alignment and your essence. You don't have to give up what you love because the economy has changed, or because you think it's not viable for some other reason. All you have to do is find new and exciting ways to make what you offer available to the world.

It starts with transformational thinking, and asking yourself, *What is it I can do that really highlights who I am?* Figure out what gets you excited, what you just can't stop talking about. My friend and neighbor of many years really struggled to find meaningful work. She tried so many things. I said, "Maybe these things are just not *you*." She realized that what she wanted to do most was help people—but she needed to get more specific. After twenty-eight years of marriage, she lost her husband. A few years later, she lost her son. Her courage was amazing!

Once she realized she could have a meaningful role by sharing her wisdom about grief and what she had gone through, knowing what kind of support she had lacked and making it available to others, a lightning bolt hit her and she couldn't stop talking about it. Now she inspires and counsels grieving mothers.

> *If you create an identity that's bigger than your job and expresses your essence, your scope can continue to grow in business and in every aspect of your life. This brings a higher level of wellness to humanity as a whole.*

Your passion is within you: it just needs to be identified. Some people know what it is right away; for others it needs to be coaxed out. So look for mentors you can trust to boost your process. You're never going to be personally free until you are financially free, so say yes to success, starting right where you are now. If you're older and hate technology, let that feeling go. We only hate what we don't understand. Don't be afraid to learn what you need to learn to operate successfully in today's market, even if that simply means whom to hire to do it for you. There are plenty of trustworthy resources to turn to for help—but it takes skill and experience to tease them out of 8.5 million search engine results.

Women, especially, tend to get stuck thinking we *are* our circumstances, or that we are stuck *in* them. But that is absolutely not true. All you have to do is broaden your imagination. Every woman is capable of reinvention after setbacks—and after those setbacks have taught her more about who she is. Every woman has distinct, valuable skills that can be repurposed and repackaged for expansion. If you create an identity that's bigger than your job and expresses your essence, your scope can continue to grow in business and in every aspect of your life. This brings a higher level of wellness to humanity as a whole.

Your possibilities are endless. Decide what they are and which audience you will serve. Gather your mentors, resources and support team to solidify your plan. Then take those meaningful actions to build the life of your dreams!

After thirty years as a custom picture framer and incurable entrepreneur, Laura Ellsworth started Say Yes to Success!™—an online showcase of world-class resources to build a business from any level to any level. She also showcases art and wellness products to enhance quality of life and promote better wellness for humanity. Connect with Laura at www.LauraEllsworth.biz.

Sherah Danielle

The Health Trinity

I t's October, 2009, and I'm driving back to Regent University in Virginia Beach. I have three days left in my fall break before my thirty-page Master of Fine Arts (MFA) portfolio document is due. The darkness of night surrounds me—it's around 11:45 p.m. and nobody else is on 64E. I turn my music up to keep me company.

Before I left, my mother asked, "Sherah, are you sure you want to leave tonight? It's so late."

"Yes," I answered. My thirty-page paper loomed in the back of my mind. Although I had already begun writing it, I felt I had put it off long enough. I needed to get it done.

"Okay," she said. "You pray about it, and do whatever you feel the Lord leads you to do."

I prayed, and felt at peace with going back to Virginia.

I stop at 7-Eleven for snacks. As I get back on the road, an image flashes through my mind: my Mercury Mountaineer, overturned by the side of the road. I see myself in an accident. I've always had a vivid imagination, which played a part in my decision to be a filmmaker.

Since I write, I often imagine different scenes for films and plays in great detail, and these scenes will come to mind in any random moment of inspiration. So I don't give any thought to the image. Instead I keep on driving, into the night.

A sudden movement on my left catches my eye, and I swerve to avoid the creature that dashes in front of my mid-sized SUV. But I turn too far, and am headed into the trees. I swerve again to avoid the trees, and again I've turned too hard. Before I know it, my SUV is flipping over. I close my eyes and scream a simple prayer: "Jesus! Jesus! Jesus!" When I open them again, I'm facing the asphalt and the car is still flipping. I see the highway from upside down, hear the sound of shattering glass, and close my eyes and shield my face from the flying glass with my arms. The car flips three times before it lands, at a diagonal, in the middle of the two-lane highway.

I have to get out of the car. What if something is leaking? The door is smashed and won't budge. And I can't get my bruised limbs to work properly so I can lift myself out a window. Then I see the bright lights of an eighteen-wheeler headed straight toward me. The truck is huge. It can't go left to get around me; it can't go right to get around me. I'm sure this is the end. As I watch the lights get closer and closer, my mind goes blank. I've already prayed. I've already screamed. I've already tried to get out. Now all I can do is wait.

Suddenly a miracle occurs. The truck squeals to a stop right in front of me, and the driver jumps out and runs to my SUV. It all happens so fast I don't even realize he has stopped—he is suddenly at my door, struggling to help pull me through a window. My left shoe has come off in the accident, and it takes me a few minutes to realize I have walked through broken glass to get to the side of the road and my foot is bleeding. I use the truck driver's cell phone to call my mother after he calls an ambulance—my own phone is somewhere in the SUV and I'm too shaken up to stand in the middle of the road to try to find it.

As the EMTs lift me onto a stretcher, I hear them grunting from bearing my weight. I am so ashamed, I feel like my heart is about to tear into pieces. I start to cry. As I ride in the ambulance, I think, *If I died, would my family and friends know that I loved them? I never even had the opportunity to live life to its fullest. I was never married, never had kids....*

I'm not where I wanted to be, by now. I wanted to be healthy. I wanted to have let go of all this extra weight.

At the ER, nurses lift me from the stretcher and again, they grunt. Humiliated, I pray that the truck driver told my mother where the ambulance was taking me—she is a whole two hours away. Lying on a gurney, I see the ceiling tiles rush by above my head. I'm so scared—I don't know where I am. I've never been in this hospital before. Looking for injuries, nurses cut the clothes from my body. I'm not in a private room. I can only make them out through my peripheral vision, but I know there are other patients all around me.

The nurse is trying to hook me up to an IV. I don't know if she is new, or what—but she sticks the needle into my arm and

> *Even before this accident, I realized that I wasn't going about weight loss in the right way.*

can't get a vein. Sticks it in, can't find a vein. The EMTs already tried in the ambulance without success. My body aches—I feel like screaming. The third time it doesn't work, I hear her say, "I can't find a vein because she has so many stretch marks." My heart is crushed. This isn't the first time I've struggled with my weight—it's been a lifelong issue.

When I was in high school, I went from over 190 pounds to 135 pounds in five months. After three years, I gained it all back. Then, when I was at Howard University, I went from over 205 pounds to 165, also in five months. Every time I yo-yo and gain the weight back, extra comes with it. I can't figure out why I'm unable to keep the weight off. As I search for the answer, I pray and talk to God, and gather wisdom from my mom.

Even before this accident, I realized that I wasn't going about weight loss in the right way. I wasn't going at it the *full* way. In other areas of my life, when I need to excel, what do I do? I pray and ask God for wisdom, and get support from my family and friends.

Wow! I seek God and pray to God in these other contexts—I need to do that with my weight. I get emotional support, soul support, from my family and friends with all kinds of projects—why not with getting healthy and finally letting go of the weight?

I'd gotten so excited about this revelation that I decided to do my MFA portfolio project about it, making a documentary involving people from all over the world who would journey with me to whole fitness. I love to help and encourage others—it is my greatest purpose. I make it a point to say to someone, every day, "Has anyone reminded you today that Jesus loves you?" But have I really reminded myself of that fact lately?

The accident leaves me depressed. My goals for school have to change—because of my injuries, my neck is in a brace and I can't even use my hands to type. People from around the world were excited to be part of the documentary journey, but those plans

It is so beautifully symmetrical: a trinity.
The Health Trinity.

now have to shift. I think I'm letting them down. I let my mother down when I dismissed my premonition of the accident—I should have just gone home. And I'm letting *everyone* down by continuing to gain weight. I'm unworthy to be the poster child for my own project.

Then the a-ha moment comes. I just need to follow the path I had been so excited about before I had the accident! It is so beautifully symmetrical: a trinity. The Health Trinity. Each aspect of fitness—spiritual (my relationship with God), soul-emotional (my relationship with my loved ones) and physical (my relationship with my body)—can support the others, and each aspect is also totally necessary for optimum well-being. There is no way I can get in shape without leaning on God and my family for support. And I can be the healthiest person in the world, but if I don't have soul-emotional fitness, I won't have loved ones around me as I'm aging. If I have soul-emotional fitness but am living without physical fitness, I may not be able to engage with the loved ones I do have at the highest possible level.

I share all this with my mother, who has been ministering to me and encouraging me my entire life. She lives The Health Trinity; it is a blessing for me to see her do it, every single day. So I seek her wisdom on how to apply it. I continue my daily devotions, and talking to the Lord every day. I always want to make sure I am growing spiritually, and that I take time out for my family. So my first practice of soul-emotional fitness has been to call or send a message to a family member, friend, or loved one at least once a week.

I'm still working toward total mobility. But I'm able to do more now than I was, say, five months ago. The weight is finally starting to come off, and this time, because the process feels like a transformation from the inside out, and I'm loving myself through it, I'm confident I can *keep* it off.

The accident and my discovery of The Health Trinity showed me what was most important to me. I need my family, friends, and loved ones. I need God. I need to make what I call "Love Time" with them and with myself, every day. By God's grace, mercy

> *You can do anything you put your spirit, soul and body (mind) to. With God, all things are possible!*

and favor, I had spiritual and soul-emotional fitness to help me through while my physical body was healing, and I have them now as I embark on the path of finally claiming my body and treating it as the temple God bestowed on me.

You can do anything you put your spirit, soul and body (mind) to. With God, all things are possible! The first step is to take time once a day to reflect on where you are and where you want to be— and thank God that you see where you *used* to be. You've made progress, even if it seems small. Being grateful for what you have is something you can always do *right now* as far as spiritual fitness—

and nurturing what you do have will help you use it to help and encourage others. Working on soul-emotional fitness can be as simple as sending a message to someone you haven't talked to in a while, giving someone a hug, saying I love you—small things you can do daily to make changes in your life and the lives of your loved ones.

Be real with yourself. If you feel you don't have time to work out, ask yourself, "Why?" Why *don't* you deserve that "Love Time?" Pray for support and guidance from God, and look to your friends and family to encourage you as you make the leap to health, even if it starts with baby steps. None of us can do it alone.

The Health Trinity is a process. It's not a fitness program, it's a lifestyle—something we cultivate daily. When we give ourselves the love and reverence we deserve, we'll be just fine. God has given us everything we need to keep on keeping on.

Sherah Danielle is a writer, director, actor, singer, photographer and producer. She is the winner of a "Miss Congeniality" title and the Paul Robeson Award for "Best Producer" in 2008. In May, 2009, two commercials that she wrote, directed and co-produced premiered in over thirty million households. She received her BFA from Howard University, and is currently completing her MFA at Regent University in film directing. Sherah is passionate about MakeRoom4Jesus.com, a movement founded by her mother, Dr. Emma Jean Thompson. Her goal is to use The Health Trinity, and her gifts in the arts and media, to help others and further the Gospel of Jesus Christ. Connect with Sherah at www.SherahDanielle.com.

Joan Cameron

The Depth of Belief

Whenever I was asked, "What do you do?" I always answered, "I work for Hewlett-Packard." After twenty years, I had become very successful as an executive, and my corporate job defined my identity; my social life revolved around my friends at work, and the time I took for myself varied or was rendered nonexistent according to the demands of the workplace. It was my whole life.

Despite my success, everything felt like a massive struggle, and my stress levels were out of control. Life was flat and joyless. The last several years I'd watched myself age dramatically. My stomach problems were constant, often leaving me curled in a ball of pain under my desk. Doctors couldn't figure out what was wrong.

At forty, I set the intention to retire by the time I was forty-five. So when my forty-fifth birthday rolled around and I was still there, I was deeply depressed. We were in the midst of downsizing and I knew I would have to start picking people to lay off. Two months later, I woke up in the middle of the night to a voice practically yelling in my head: "I'm going to take the cut! I'm going to volunteer myself and quit!"

I see it now as divine guidance—myself, my own spirit crying out to me: "Hey! It's time. End this chapter and move on to a new one. Create a new life of meaning and joy." For me, there was no other choice. I knew if I stayed in my job for another five, ten years, the stress would kill me. And then there was the matter of the corporate soul, whose ugly reflection was making me literally ill. Every day I had to make decisions that I knew, deep down, were not right. So I quit.

Just like that. I got exactly the amount of money I had hoped for, the umbrella package, the stock, the parachute, the whole thing, down to the dollar. This was a significant insight to the power of imagination and intention, and how the universe aligns with them.

Still, I was hanging on to a false identity. For months after I quit, when people asked, "What do you do?" I continued to answer

I see it now as divine guidance—myself, my own spirit crying out to me: "Hey! It's time. End this chapter and move on to a new one. Create a new life of meaning and joy."

that I had worked for Hewlett-Packard. I didn't know what else to say. My identity had been stripped away, but I had not yet found a self to replace it with. The pivotal moment came when once again, I was asked, "What do you do?"

I stood there in silence for a moment. And then I replied: "Nothing."

That is when my life changed. That was my awakening. Since I was starting from scratch, I realized I could create whoever I wanted to be and whatever life I wanted! I began searching for answers on how to re-create myself and overcome the many physical problems I had developed from years of stress and sports. Then I read *Biology of Beliefs,* by Bruce H. Lipton, PhD. He described how our beliefs, not our genes, are the key to life. I read further and found that beliefs not only played a huge factor in my health, they were creating my entire life.

I discovered the power of my mind and what I was unconsciously creating through my beliefs. I'd been a very competitive gymnast, swimmer and cyclist. My beliefs included, *I must be bone-skinny to be a top athlete,* and *No pain, no gain.* These beliefs expressed themselves in a compulsive athleticism that battered my body and my self-confidence.

By the time I was forty, my knees were in such bad shape I could hardly walk. I had already had four knee surgeries, and after the last, the doctor said I would need another in about seven years. Scared to death, I took up yoga. My knees were fine for exactly seven

That is when my life changed. That was my awakening. Since I was starting from scratch, I realized I could create whoever I wanted to be and whatever life I wanted!

years—and then I started having terrible pain again. I thought, *What's the matter? I've been doing nothing to stress this knee.* And then I realized: *Oh my gosh, the doctor said I would need surgery again in seven years. That's now!* I started looking for surgeons.

This is when I learned more from Dr. Lipton and realized that my mind, and the belief that I would need surgery, had created a painful knee! The medical term for this is the "Nocebo Effect," the power of negative beliefs. I had heard of the power of positive thoughts, the concept of mind over matter and the term "Placebo Effect," but now I was living a real nightmare. I had picked up negative beliefs from my doctor and created pain in my knee. My next question was, how do I change these beliefs and avoid another knee surgery?

Dr. Lipton recommended PSYCH-K® as his chosen process to change beliefs, including the foundational ones we all hold at the subconscious level. I flew to Denver to learn PSYCH-K®, and started changing my limiting subconscious beliefs to life-enhancing ones after just two days of training. The process was much easier than I ever thought it would be, and it satisfied my critical business mind, which demands results. I began using my new skills to create who I wanted to be through my beliefs and quickly became more calm, peaceful and happy. The results were so life-changing that I decided to become a PSYCH-K® instructor.

That was about four years ago, and I've never needed surgery. I'm happily sprinting up and down the thirty-one steps in my house; I feel confident in my body and even regularly do a yoga posture I avoided trying for four years. Instead of the voice in my head saying, *You're going to get hurt,* I feel gratitude and love for my knees. Wow! These knees took me over twenty-five-thousand miles on my bike.

When I re-programmed my limiting beliefs, I took my foot off the brake and the knee pain went away! When I learned these new skills, I started creating according to what I wanted to have instead of this painful knee. I re-programmed my subconscious mind, the part that holds our beliefs in long-term memory and runs them on auto-pilot. I created such beliefs as: *My knees are healthy and strong. My body heals itself naturally. I love my knees.* I'd hated my knees since they dislocated when I was thirteen. A part of me was this belief that they were always failing me, and this belief was playing over and over in my head until it became true! My new goal was to love, trust and be grateful for my knees.

What I found was not only a way to create the life of my dreams, but also a way to help others in any area of their life. A woman who came to me for support with her divorce discovered her own limiting beliefs kept her from seeing the love in her husband's eyes and the blessings in their marriage. She ended up staying happily married and learned PSYCH-K® so that she could keep the fire burning.

One of my favorite sayings is one from Mahatma Gandhi: "Keep your beliefs positive, because your beliefs become your thoughts, your thoughts become your words, your words become your actions, your actions become your habits, your habits become your values and your values become your destiny." Inspired and self-empowered, I have created the life of my dreams through my beliefs. I have my own business where I inspire and teach people around the world—Egypt, New Zealand, Central America, the United States—to discover and live their greatness through their beliefs. I am fulfilling a life-long dream of exotic travel, making a difference in the world, and making a living doing it!

Beliefs set the limits to what we can achieve. Our common—and most profoundly limiting—core belief is that we are disconnected from a divine source. This belief keeps us separate from our power and who we truly are, like a layer around our divinity that must be peeled away to find the jewel in the middle. I grew up thinking I had to do, do, do in order to be loved, when unconditional love is my birthright. I learned that I am not defined by what I do, what I achieve: I am divine just as I am.

> I learned that I am not defined by what I do, what I achieve: I am divine just as I am.

You can tap into your own wisdom and become your own healer, the creator of your own life, one belief at a time. Here is one process I use: First, write down a problem, such as, "I'm not happy in my job and I feel stuck." Then ask yourself, "What would I rather have instead?" (When I really think about what I want, sometimes I realize I never even thought about it; instead, I just kept reinforcing the same old negative message.) Then, write down what you want, for example: "I'd like to really feel passionate about my work, feel fulfilled, happy, and I'd like to make a difference in the world."

Next, create a belief declaration. Make it first person, present tense, positive, short, and emotionally compelling, like "I feel passionate about my work." "I'm fulfilled, happy and I make a difference in the world." Now *that's* getting energy moving in the right direction!

The philosopher J. Krishnamurti said, "What you are, the world is. And without your transformation there can be no transformation of the world." As quantum physics has shown, our beliefs radiate from us, feeding the collective consciousness.

If I want to transform the world, it starts with me. I focus on peeling away my layers of limiting beliefs to reveal the true, divine me—a person filled with love, abundance, gratitude and peace. This is what I'm feeding the collective consciousness, and how I'm changing the world, one belief at a time.

These days, when I'm asked, "What do you do?" my answer explains who I am, rather than what I do. I am a divine being having an extraordinary human experience. I live my life filled with passion and love.

Who are you? Join me on this enchanted journey. The world needs your transformation.

Joan Cameron is the founder of Your Beliefs Matter, an international, heart-based self-empowerment-training company teaching individuals and groups skills and processes to reach their highest potential in life. She's an inspirational speaker, workshop leader and writer, and offers e-trainings and other online tools for self-transformation including the Love Your Life Mastery Series and PSYCH-K®. Her humanitarian efforts take her to help children with hiv/aids in Guatemala, to a girls' orphanage in Nicaragua, to the Maori prison system in New Zealand, and to Oregon and Washington. Joan lived in Germany during the fall of the Berlin Wall, speaks German, is learning Spanish, and has traveled to more than thirty countries. She lives in Portland, Oregon, and part-time in Nicaragua. Connect with Joan at www.YourBeliefsMatter.com.

Barbara Wirth

New Career Chameleon

Oh, come on, ring, I commanded my phone, impatiently. *Surely someone out there can use my thirty-five years of professional interior design expertise.* Seemingly not: the phone stayed quiet.

In a recession, many successful self-employed consultants were facing a similar crisis, neither thriving nor surviving. Suddenly, the career I'd built with such care—the career I truly loved—was no longer in high demand. Interior design was considered a luxury in a volatile economic climate. I had three options: (one) wait, and hope things improved; (two) be creative, and follow a new career path; or (three) call it a day, and retire.

The word "hope" implies passivity; retiring felt like giving up. Okay, that left option number two. *It was time to be innovative, as innovative as a chameleon,* I thought. Chameleons are fascinating creatures. Without changing their identity, they adapt to their surroundings simply by changing color. They are masters of survival. "If they can do it, why couldn't I? In fact, I'll become a new career chameleon."

Just saying it gave me a lift, although what I was going to do next remained a mystery. Since change and mystery can be threats to our comfort zones, I have to admit to mental heel-dragging. Reasons "why not" to change flooded my brain. Have you ever felt that way? It's easy to pinpoint what's not working, but answering, "How do I change it?" is tricky.

I then asked myself a simple question: *What aspects of interior design do I like best?* My answer included creativity, color, seeing a stylish transformation and helping others enjoy their homes even more. Where and how could I use these passions in a new profession? I got my answer in a surprising way—but first, let me backtrack a little.

Several months before my phone stopped ringing, I spent a memorable Saturday with thirty other women in a collaboration day of meditation, yoga and art. I remember how free, almost childlike, I felt. As I was leaving, Sandy Hersh, one of the event

> *It's easy to pinpoint what's not working, but answering, "How do I change it?" is tricky.*

creators, and a very talented artist herself, called me aside. "Barbara," she asked, with her eyes fixed on mine and her hand on my shoulder, "when are you going to start painting again?" Although I replied with a dismissive, "Oh, I don't know," I knew her question was sincere and somehow profound. Indeed, this encouraging exchange planted a seed of inspiration.

A little while later, at a garden-gallery event, I met Wanda Avery, an inspirational artist. She mixes pen and ink with watercolors— and the result is art I consider to be absolutely stunning. Over glasses of iced tea, we exchanged appreciation for each other's talent. Color me flattered when she invited me to paint with her art group. With paintbrush in hand and pure joy in my heart, I was soon painting in earnest—and once again, I felt liberated and childlike. It felt so good that I converted part of my home into a studio.

During a later conversation, my very good friend, Lilly Emerson, revealed how twice she had searched high and low for a journal to take on her recent trips to Tonga and Peru. "Since they were to be very memorable trips for me," she said reflectively, "I'd have given anything to find journals that featured your watercolors—with plenty of lined pages for me to write on, plus plenty of blank pages for me to scrapbook-on-the-go."

Hmm, I thought. *Is this an aha moment? I'm certainly feeling a sense of stimulation.* Yet I still could not complete the puzzle. The following Monday, I returned to my office. By now, I was checking to make sure the phone had not turned into a moldy mushroom from lack of use. I was suddenly aware of a conflict raging within me.

Why was I sitting in my office *hoping* for business when I could be *doing* something new and amazing in my studio instead? Up until this moment, my business had remained interior design, and my newly rediscovered painting was pure pleasure.

I sat quietly. I dug deep into my heart and listened respectfully to my uncensored thoughts and feelings. My earlier aha moment now became my turning point. Not only did I need to use my

> *Satisfaction, on the other hand, comes when we've not only developed our talents but also shared them. The greatest reward for me comes from knowing I've made a positive difference in someone else's life.*

talents in a different way, I also recognized that I needed a recipient for them. We all have our own areas of expertise, and developing them is vital to personal growth. Satisfaction, on the other hand, comes when we've not only developed our talents but also shared them. The greatest reward for me comes from knowing I've made a positive difference in someone else's life.

Lilly's wishful thinking about having a "journal with your artwork and blank pages for mine" suddenly resonated, loud and clear. Surely, she wasn't the only creative person who craved such a journal. Millions of people throughout the world must be anxious to capture the experiences and beauty of their travels. All they needed was the actual journal. I could do that!

Indeed, this project matched and surpassed my criteria. Would designing and producing such a journal involve creativity, color, seeing a stylish transformation and adding to others' enjoyment? Absolutely yes! Moreover, there was a ready-made market of enthusiastic recipients. My passions now had purpose, color, texture, weight and shape—and I felt elated.

Ironically, the more I painted, and the more journal designs and sizes I considered, the more my phone rang. Energy *does* create energy, and each time the phone rang, I knew I'd chosen the right "next step" in life.

Months later, I have two creative travel journals and more offered on my website. I'm exploring the many marketing possibilities for the travel journals, as well as a range of other innovative journals everyone can use and enjoy. It's a great strategic adventure. I'm alive again, and yes, my phone is almost as busy as I am these days.

> *Stay connected to the voice that said, "You can." Borrow from that person's confidence in you. Tap into it.*

People are interested in my career change. My story is simply a reflection of the crossroads so many other professionals are facing. It's caught its fair share of media attention as well, and appearing on business chat shows is a stimulating, enjoyable new experience for me. Some have described my decision as "courageous." My perspective is different.

During my transformation, I certainly questioned my path, but only briefly. I found I could easily replace that hesitation with excitement. I never left myself floating in a bubble of indecision where it would have been easy to look backwards and get frustrated, thinking about what I no longer had. I was never in that place of, "Oh my gosh, I don't have that anymore." In that, I am blessed.

I know not everyone is able to avoid the paralysis. When I was on the edge of it, I'd just remember the voice of the person, or people, who said, "You'd be great at doing that," and that remembrance would kick me into action. But for those who have a harder time accessing that I-can-do attitude, I would recommend that you return to those original voices of inspiration, those people who said you can do it, and ask them, "How? You said I can do it, but how do you see me doing it?" Stay connected to the voice that said, "You can." Borrow from that person's confidence in you. Tap into it.

And then there are those who can't even hear the compliments, even as they're being showered upon them. I know the type. It's okay. For those of you who think no one is complimenting you, no one has identified a singular strength in you, do this. Go to someone you respect and ask, "What is special about me? What makes me unique?" After the "what" question, ask the "how" question, and be open to hearing the answers.

Turning life's lemons into lemonade is a soul-searching challenge. But we're given plenty of guidance along the way. We simply have to pay attention to our situations; acknowledge our talents; ask powerful, personal questions; and honor those key people who give our goals definition, direction and support. Once I noticed, once I listened and expressed gratitude, I was able to move from disappointment in my dormant career to the exhilaration I'm feeling in my new one.

In fact, just like the resourceful chameleon, my career colors have changed from disappointing browns and grays to a sunburst of yellows, purples, blues, reds—and any other colors I may add to the mix!

Career-change chameleon Barbara Wirth has gone from being a successful interior designer to designing and producing exquisite travel journals. She and her husband, Cary Wirth, founded Travel Legacy®, a company that is changing the way we record and recall our journeys. Connect with Barbara at www.TravelLegacy.net.

Ruby Yeh

Living Heaven on Earth

Y ou ask, and you receive. You wake up happy, really, truly happy. Your life just flows. Even when life presents challenges, you don't worry. You know everything will work out exactly as it should. You call forth feelings of absolute love and peace at a moment's notice. You are protected. Doors open for you, seats are saved for you, time waits for you. When you are a little late to the airport, the plane is delayed. When you think of something or someone, that something or someone shows up.

Living your heart's desire is not a pipe dream, or even a secret wish; it is totally natural and it is available now. What is this life I describe? It is grace beyond words. It is heaven on earth.

Henry David Thoreau said, "Most men lead lives of quiet desperation and go to the grave with the song still in them." I never bought into that. I was determined that would never happen to me. After college I set out on a spiritual quest for the secret to real and true happiness. Real and true happiness, that which cannot be taken from you, that which does not break in the storm, or even bend in the wind.

This was not a small task—and I didn't go about it like some people who give up their "normal" lives to discover themselves. I did it while climbing the corporate ladder in Fortune 500 America and as an entrepreneur in Silicon Valley.

In the competitive world of business, I worked collaboratively, and as a result I experienced a lot of external success. I had "everything:" a great international career in Fortune 500 America, a loving boyfriend, great experiences traveling around the globe. But none of this could provide real and true happiness; I knew that. So I continued to be devoted to my spiritual quest.

I took hundreds of workshops, read a lot, and learned much about emotional intelligence, psychology, spirituality and Eastern philosophy. It was a long, hard slog. It was literally three steps forward, two steps back, and being burned in many cauldron fires

Henry David Thoreau said, "Most men lead lives of quiet desperation and go to the grave with the song still in them." I never bought into that. I was determined that would never happen to me.

of "deep dark nights of the soul." But still, I kept on. I sometimes joke that I am really a monk who is merely masquerading as an entrepreneur.

Then one June night, I decided to check out "The Hugging Saint" while she was visiting the San Francisco area. Amma, as she is known today, is a spiritual leader and humanitarian who has hugged more than twenty-six million people worldwide. My first spiritual teacher was a guru from India, so the chanting and stories that evening were familiar to me. But I never liked any of the Eastern rituals, so when I got in line for my hug from Amma and someone asked me if I would like a mantra, I surprised myself by saying, "Yes."

When Amma hugged me, it felt nice, but nothing out of the ordinary happened. And receiving the mantra, while interesting, was also nothing special. I felt a lot of energy in the room that night, but having spent years searching for real and true happiness and never quite finding it, I dismissed it as a "group high" from all of the chanting.

Just as I was getting up to leave, a blonde woman in a beautiful sari turned to me and said, "You should stay. The morning ceremony is extraordinary. It is Mother revealing and gracing us with the Divine Mother energy." Curious, I stayed, curled up and fell asleep in a corner of the room. When the morning ceremony began, the blonde devotee ushered me to the front of the room, near Amma. Being so close to her, feeling her energy, my heart burst open with a flood of joyful tears. It was truly indescribable.

Even though I wrote off my ecstatic experience as "a momentary spiritual high," I started conducting "spiritual research" about Amma. I read many books about her. I "interviewed" devotees about their experiences and how their lives have changed. I wanted practical, real-world examples of how their lives improved after meeting her, not a bunch of starry-eyed, woo-woo talk. I was moved by their stories of Amma's infinite compassion and the

I sometimes joke that I am really a monk who is merely masquerading as an entrepreneur.

miracles she brought into their lives. A professional woman who regularly tours with her told me, "Since Amma, I have no fear in my life." I thought, *I want some of that!*

Still, I was skeptical. I had traveled the world, devoted years of my life to searching for real and true happiness. For two and a half years I studied Amma, went to see her when she came to town twice a year and learned all I could about her. I was fascinated by how this woman with a fourth-grade education was able to run charitable operations that handled hundreds of millions of dollars per year, including the hospitals, universities and dozens of other humanitarian operations she founded, while also touching so many millions around the world with her motherly hugs every year.

Through this time period I was also looking after my ailing mother, which took a toll on me physically, emotionally and financially. During some really trying times, I decided to experiment by turning to Amma, since I didn't have anything to lose by asking for her help. I was amazed that I felt better even if the circumstances didn't change right away. And oftentimes, my external situation did improve!

I even started chanting the mantra in my head when I needed relief from my own worrying mind. Gradually I came to understand that Amma was my connection to Spirit, to real and true happiness. Wrapped in her infinite embrace at all times, I became awash in boundless, unconditional love.

In the protection of her omniscient power, I am safe. Her compassion and unconditional love free my soul to be truly happy. Amma sees all that I am and all that I can be, and I am limitless. I am my own heart's desire, my own heaven on earth. She blesses me, and I know my quest is over. At last, I have found my spiritual home, and I fall fully into the nectar of Amma's love.

> *When we connect to Spirit, every-thing is love and all is possible, because Spirit protects us, hears our prayers, answers our requests, sees us for who we really are and loves us no matter what.*

What is the source of infinite strength, energy and joy? It is connection to Spirit. Without this connection, we perceive ourselves as limited, cut off from true happiness, from our heart's desires. When we connect to Spirit, everything is love and all is possible, because Spirit protects us, hears our prayers, answers our requests, sees us for who we really are and loves us no matter what.

For me, that connection to Spirit is through Amma. I searched my whole life to find it, and when I finally allowed my rational mind to follow my heart's wisdom, I came to experience what it really truly means to be happy. I can honestly say I lead a joyful life. I literally wake up happy and feeling blessed every day. Even when I'm tired, or working through challenges, or dealing with unknowns, I am happy. I don't get stressed. Why should I? When you have Spirit or "the biggest cheese of all time" on your side, what can go wrong?

The moment I wake up, I feel the presence of Spirit embracing me. I feel Spirit's guidance, protection and favor. And because I feel this, of course I can move forward with inspiration and excitement. Of course I am happy. Of course I am blessed. What a joy it is to have Spirit's protection and favor upon me every day!

If you haven't yet connected to Spirit, you can begin by just asking for what you need or want. You can also connect by getting out of your mind and dropping into your heart and body.

I carry this energy with me throughout the day. It's funny—people sometimes remark that I am always "doing, doing, doing, always focused and on the go," but I don't feel behind, or pressured, or stressed. It all feels effortless.

Rather than being anxious about life, I allow opportunities and experiences to flow into my life. I literally magnetize what I need, and what I desire. Everything just shows up. It shows up because I simply ask.

Every day, I ask Amma how I can best serve the world through my passion dance and the use of the skills and resources I have been blessed with. I ask for inspiration, vision, positive outcomes, the fulfillment of every wish, and Amma leads me to my heart's desires. She does this because she is a Divine Mother, and every mother wants her children to be happy. This is Spirit, and Spirit, in whatever form, is available to all of us. We must simply ask, and we will most assuredly receive.

We're at the feast table that is life, but most of us crawl around on the floor picking up crumbs when we could simply ask to sit at the table. Spirit loves me, Spirit loves you, Spirit loves everyone and wants all of us to live in joy. Yet we rarely just ask. Why would you think that the "biggest cheese of all time" can't fulfill your desires? Why not? Spirit can do whatever it wants, and Spirit will always fulfill my heart's true desires and your heart's wishes. That is what Spirit does.

After years of searching, I can honestly say that I have achieved sustained peace and joy. For me, this is because of my connection to Spirit through Amma, but she is not the only doorway to this life, this heaven on earth. What is your connection to Spirit? Is it through Jesus, your religion, your God, a guru or teacher, or through nature? If you haven't yet connected to Spirit, you can begin by just asking for what you need or want. You can also connect by getting out of your mind and dropping into your heart and body.

I create my own "joy juice" by simply falling back into my heart, and letting that feeling of bliss radiate throughout my body. I can do it anywhere—in my car, in a room full of people, anywhere—simply by relaxing and focusing my attention on my heart and body. It feels like I'm floating in my own personal nectar soup. My whole body feels awesome, a sense of electrified, sweet softness.

You can do this, too. You can create your own "joy juice" just by settling into your body, falling back into your heart and letting the love fill up every inch of you. Like a hug from Amma, or whatever you connect to, whomever you are devoted to.

When we are in connection to Spirit, we experience Spirit's favor, protection and love. This is the source of real, true happiness. It is possible to experience heaven on earth. Don't lead a "life of quiet desperation." Find your connection to Spirit, to Grace, and let it carry you, gently and lovingly, to your heart's desires.

Ruby Yeh is the Founder of Yinspire Media, a new media publishing company and the private-brand publishing partner behind recent bestselling books by industry superstars Lisa Nichols and Les Brown. Ruby pioneered next-generation, experiential reading through multimedia books that come alive with text, audio and video for computers, iPads and iPhones. She leverages her background as a Fortune 500 marketing executive and Silicon Valley entrepreneur to help visionaries catapult their message to the global market and develop lucrative "info-preneur" businesses.

Ruby has helped more than three hundred Yinspire Media authors to be published in cutting-edge new media books, and bestselling authors of traditional print books. She is the partner for eWomenPublishingNetwork, a division of eWomen Network Inc., one of the country's largest networks for female entrepreneurs; eWomen Publishing Network is a world-class team of publishing, marketing and social media experts that coaches entrepreneurs, speakers and aspiring and established authors on how to develop their star power as industry authorities. Connect with Ruby at www.YinspireMedia.com and www.AliveEBooks.com.

To learn more about Amma's teachings and humanitarian activities, visit www.Amma.org.

Pamela Zimmer

Extraordinarily Normal

Do you ever wonder if, compared to the big goals others pursue, what you want seems too ordinary, too easy, too—normal? Working women often hear about certain risks: starting a new career; changing careers; or moving from one city to another for our careers. But leaving our careers to become stay-at-home moms is rarely discussed. Not only is this as big a risk as the others, it's also a risk women often consider.

I believe part of why we don't discuss this is because people think being a stay-at-home mom is so normal, so average. I believe some people think being a stay-at-home mom holds little or no value compared to having a working career. This can especially be the case among us career women who have spent our lives trying to excel at something that will make us exceptional.

"Normal" and "average" can bring such huge amounts of happiness that they are not normal or average at all. And just because a lot of people are doing something, such as being stay-at-home moms, doesn't mean it isn't an exceptional thing to do.

My story isn't solely about becoming a stay-at-home mom. What it's really about is me making a big change to align with my transformation: How I did it, and how you can do it, too. Even before I got married and had children, I wanted to be a stay-at-home mom. Part of my inspiration was my own mother. She was a nurse, and she worked nights. She was there to make dinner and put us to bed, and she was there when my sister and I woke up, so it seemed she was always there. As my sister and I got older, she quit her job so she could literally always be there for us. She did that because she wanted to.

I also had this strong ambition and drive to be a successful businesswoman. My mother once told me that when I wanted something, I focused on my goal until I achieved it. And in business, I achieved my goal: I became a successful architect with my own firm. And yet, throughout the process, I often beat myself up, saying, "Why did I even start this firm, knowing I want to be

> *My story isn't solely about becoming a stay-at-home mom. What it's really about is me making a big change to align with my transformation: How I did it, and how you can do it, too.*

a stay-at-home mom?" It felt as though a string was pulling me in two totally opposite directions, one side attached to my head, the other to my heart.

On September 15, 2007, I gave birth to our first son, Zackery Gendebien Zimmer. I gave birth naturally through hypnobirthing, and it was amazing. I was so proud of the birth, and I literally cried every time I looked at our new baby. My husband, Will, wasn't working at the time, so initially we were both able to stay home. After three months, I had to return to work, and that's when the yearning to be home with Zack became incredibly strong—a one-ton chain attached to my heart, pulled by a bulldozer.

I returned to work four days a week, and Will often brought Zack in for a long lunch or an afternoon visit. It was still hard. I left for work each morning, but I really wanted to just stay at home and be present with my son. I got a lump in my throat every time I had to leave, and the tears flowed more and more. I couldn't sleep at night, and my body was tense all day.

I felt so dull and lifeless, like a cardboard figure on a board game in someone else's world. I was jealous when my husband called and told me what he and Zack were doing. I wanted to be happy because I knew Will was trying to keep me involved, but it wasn't enough. I knew that I needed to make a big change if I wanted to be happy and fill the void in my heart.

To make a change, you have to be completely clear about what you want. It's not enough to simply be unhappy in your situation. You cannot work toward what you want if you don't know what that is. In getting clear about what I wanted, I asked myself, *What really makes me happy? What fills up my heart?* It took time and energy to figure it out, but once I realized that I needed to be a stay-at-home mom, it became easier to focus on my goal. What's more, once I truly got clear and started saying it out loud, even to myself, things began to align, and I felt my life getting back on track.

My business partner knew that eventually I wanted to have another baby, and that when I did, I wanted to be a stay-at-home mom, then. I told him we needed to figure out a two-year exit plan for me to leave the company. I also told my husband what I wanted to do, and together, we began to work toward it.

Once you're crystal clear on what you want, the crucial next step is to tell other people and get their support. Not everyone will be supportive. When I told other people that I was leaving my business after my second son was born, they asked, "For how long? Three months?"

When I said, "No, it's permanent," they often said, "You're crazy." I even got that from other working mothers. Comments like those made me want to shout out loud so they would understand. Sometimes I kept my plans to myself for fear of people's reactions. However, I stuck to my goal and surrounded myself with people who supported me.

My husband was immediately supportive. I felt blessed to have a husband who trusted me, had faith in me and knew this was going to be good for our whole family. I felt warm and light inside, like he was giving my heart a big, giant hug. I believe that's what family is all about. Family, real family, is with you through the good and the bad, the easy and the hard, the past and the future. Family is forever.

Without my dad, I would not feel the pride I know he has in me. Without my sister, I would not have anyone to share the truly precious moments of growing up together, from girls into women. Without my sons, I would not have such heartfelt tears of joy, love and pure laughter. My mother is up above, looking over me every second, and without her I would not have become the beautiful, loving and caring woman that she always was.

I believe so many families automatically choose to put their kids in daycare and go back to work because they think it's what they're expected to do. When it comes to your dreams, don't let society

> *When we don't listen to our hearts, we become unhappy. And the less happy we are, the less happy we make those around us.*

make your decisions. There is a time for making choices with your head, but you must also let your heart have a voice. When we don't listen to our hearts, we become unhappy. And the less happy we are, the less happy we make those around us.

I often wonder how much better our world might be if we all followed our hearts. If a mother wants to stay home to care for her newborn, why shouldn't our society support her?

Why, as women, do we have the burden of choosing between our families and careers?

How does my family benefit from me going back to work after three months, or even six weeks?

And if my family isn't the best it can be, how does that help society? I'm not naïve. I know there are legitimate financial consequences to making big changes. I faced those myself. Sometimes, we have to follow our heads. For me, I knew that I wouldn't ever truly be happy if I kept letting my head get in the way. I had to figure a way to put my heart before my head.

Another key in successfully transforming my life was taking baby steps. I'm an average person, and I think a lot of people are like me. I hear stories about people who overcame really horrible things to be incredibly successful, and I think, *Great, but that's not my story.* Fortunately, most of us haven't had something awful happen. To make my transformation, I didn't have to overcome

> *I am not changing who I am.*
> *I'm merely changing my conditions.*
> *When YOU make your big change, you're*
> *not changing who you are, either. You're*
> *just changing your conditions.*

anything tragic. I merely needed to change some of my external conditions, conquer the internal fear and learn to take baby steps.

By baby steps, I mean laying the groundwork for my future. I left my business one month before my second son was born, after over a year of planning and phasing out. It was one of the hardest things I ever did: My business was, essentially, my first baby. I also let go of being the local Club President for CEO Space. All of this made room for my transformation, and allowed me to once again be me. I am not changing who I am. I'm merely changing my conditions. When YOU make your big change, you're not changing who you are, either. You're just changing your conditions.

I often get introduced as an architect, but I am really so much more. To understand who you are, you need to look inside. So many people think who you are is what you do, and that's sad, especially if it makes you unhappy. What you do is just a factor of your external conditions. It is not who you are. What a relief to know who I am will always remain the same, no matter how many times I choose to change my conditions.

I changed my conditions when they stopped being enough. I listened to and followed my heart. I have always loved to write, and now that I am at home I find myself inspired again. Not only do I find joy in being with my family, but it is my purpose and passion for my family that is now manifesting as the inspiration to write again. I want to write something that will empower and inspire other women to go get what they want. I want to tell them that it's okay to make a change, and I want to support them in making that change.

I'm working toward my next goal. With each baby step, I am creating a better life. Every day, I feel a tingling rush of energy coupled with a certain calm, like I know I'm going in the right direction. I am starting the next chapter of my amazing journey. My smile widens, and my heart just oozes with love.

Even if you feel "average," like I do, you can still make an extraordinary transformation. Transformation does not have to hurt. Transformation does not require you to abandon all that you know and love. Transformation does not demand you walk through fire. All that you must do is take one small, first step. And then another. And another. *What is your first step?*

Pamela Zimmer worked in architecture for six years before opening her own firm, Gaunt-Zimmer Design, which she ran with her business partner for seven years before she left to become a stay-at-home mom to her two sons, Zackery and Brayden. She has been very active in CEO Space and spent a year as Club President for Reno, Nevada and Lake Tahoe, California. She is now dedicated to raising her sons and helping other "normal" and "average" women pursue their dreams. She is currently working on her first book. Connect with Pamela at www.DreamBelieveBe.com.

Zaida Garcia

What's Your Next Sail?

Years ago, when I was traveling and working all the time, I thought I had it all. But when my beloved dad suddenly got sick, time stopped and all other priorities were put on hold. Doctors didn't know what was wrong with him, so we brought him to the hospital for tests. After hours and hours of waiting, the doctor came out and said that my dad had three days to live. He was diagnosed with lymphoma and leukemia, a rare combination of illnesses.

Oh my God! How could this be possible? Dad had always been so healthy, so happy, so strong and muscular. Dad was our hero. He had even saved our lives, back when I was about a year old and Castro took over in Cuba. My dad's beliefs did not align with communism, so he was seen as a threat. And his first priority was his family; he wasn't going anywhere without us. We couldn't just leave the island—we had to escape, fast.

So one moonless night, my dad, my mom (six months pregnant), my little brother and I fled on a boat, leaving the rest of our family and all of our possessions behind. When the authorities realized we had left, they sent out armed boats and planes to shoot us down. My dad, Rene Garcia, was such an expert, well-known captain that he was called "Ocean Wolf." Knowing the sea like the back of his hand, he moved the boat to a place where we could not be seen.

Our escape took us through a storm that my mom calls the worst she's ever experienced. Without my father's expert hand to guide us, we would have died.

My dad loved the ocean; it was his second home. And he loved to travel. Just before he got sick, he bought an old sailboat and fixed it. He wanted to sail to Honduras to visit friends and my brother. Again, he faced a dramatic storm, and passed through it. When he sailed into the marina, the people there said, "Who brought that boat here? It's a miracle!" The boat was shredded, but he had made it! He was so happy. Though he didn't know it, it was his last sail. But even if he had, he wouldn't have let it stop him. He always lived in the moment, and did what he wanted to do without regrets.

The three days the doctors gave us passed, and then weeks, as he underwent chemo. But Dad kept his high spirits, telling friends, "I'm sick, but I feel fine." After a while, his hair fell out, he couldn't eat and was very weak. He got so thin, I hardly recognized him. He passed away a year after his diagnosis.

The experience of losing my beloved dad rocked me to my core. The question it brought up was, "What is most important to me in life?" I knew it was my family, but I realized just how much I'd left unsaid and undone with my dad, even in our last year together. I couldn't go back and say those things to him now, so how could I change? I looked at the structure of my life and saw that, in general, I had not made enough quality time for what was most precious to me.

It was a radical change. As I started peeling the onion and getting centered in my inner source, I began to discover who I really am. I looked at everything I was doing and asked myself, "Is this what I truly want for the rest of my life?"

"No," I answered back. "There are still things to be done." The loss of my dad, and remembering his character, showed me that I needed to do them *now*. Why wait? And for what? I asked myself, "What are my core values?" Then I created a system for living them to the highest degree possible. It became my mission to empower other people to live the same way.

I wanted to take time NOW—each day—to care of what was truly important. So after asking myself and interviewing experts, I came up with the five most important values: health, wealth, self, relationships and contribution. I call the tool I developed to nurture them the "Hi5." It started out very simply: once I determined the five core values, I put them in order from one to five, and then used the most obvious symbol of power—my hand—to remind myself of those values every day. I named my thumb and each finger for a value.

The thumb is strongest, so it represents health. Without health, you can't be strong in other areas. Your index finger points to others: it is your intention for contribution. The middle finger is for yourself—say "uh-uh" with that middle finger: I've got to take

> I asked myself, "What are my core values?" Then I created a system for living them to the highest degree possible. It became my mission to empower other people to live the same way.

care of *me!* I've got to be in balance so I have time for spirituality, play and everything that feeds me. The ring finger represents relationships and how you engage with family, soul-mate, friends, neighbors, co-workers and clients. The little finger is wealth—point it out and then toward you to call the outside in. Once you have the other Hi5s in place, wealth comes easily.

Every part of the Hi5 is profoundly related to LOVE—love for your health, love for your family and others, love for prosperity and, most importantly, love for thyself! Every evening I write a plan, and when I wake up each morning, I look at my hand and ask myself, "What am I doing today toward one, two, three, four, five?" At midday I check in and ask myself what I have accomplished. And before I go to sleep each night, I look at my hand again, and say my results to myself out loud. I always go to sleep with a smile on my face.

When I began simply concentrating on my Hi5, huge transformation started happening in my life. Because anything I considered doing had to connect with one of my five core values, I learned better how to speak up for myself, that what I have to say is important, and to say "no" when no was the right answer. And I noticed that when I did speak, people heard me and were inspired. If people didn't respect me, or brought negative energy into my world, I stopped allowing them into my positive, happy space.

Loving myself for who I am, a woman powerful beyond measure and able to do anything I put my mind to, I recognized I had the

> *Today, I am living my Hi5. I feel a sense of balance. I always had goals, but they were not clear. Now, every goal I set relates to what is most important to me.*

freedom to choose my extraordinary life. Then I took the bull by the horns and rode it! Like my dad, I don't let any obstacle stand in the way of living a full and loving life.

Living my Hi5, I take time every day to say what needs to be said to my family, and spend time with them. When my daughter Jenny lived in New York, and I missed her and wanted to fly to New York to be with her, I just did it.

Before, when I was working all the time, I paid no attention to my health or what I was eating. Now that it's part of my Hi5, I take care of my health each day, and I feel so good. I have so much more energy for the rest of my Hi5, including the work that I love, work that supports me in abundance, and building my contribution.

I value my own dreams, vision, drive and time alone for myself. Today, I am living my Hi5. I feel a sense of balance. I always had goals, but they were not clear. Now, every goal I set relates to what is most important to me.

Many years ago, when I first began to travel, I saw that here in the United States we really do have it all. In some parts of the world, people have nothing—no hope, no help, nowhere to turn.

When I visited Honduras, I saw whole villages of cardboard shacks with whatever could pass for roofs strapped on top. I would drive by settlements like these each day on my way to town. One day I thought, *I have to do something for these people.* I started taking my brother's truck to stores in town, where I'd buy big bags of rice and beans, plus toys and clothes for the kids, and bring it all back to the villages to distribute.

I started on my own, but I knew I needed to "not just give a man a fish, but teach him how to fish so he can feed himself for a lifetime," as the saying goes.

I've never stopped working to support others in need, or believing it's not all about me. If everyone planted a little seed, the world would be a very different place. That's why I became a

> *The other foundation of my life today, and of my coaching and training, is what I call "The 5 Goods"—feel good, look good, do good, be good and have good.*

speaker—the more transformations I help along, the more good can be done.

The other foundation of my life today, and of my coaching and training, is what I call "The 5 Goods"—feel good, look good, do good, be good and have good. When you feel good, you look good. When you look and feel good, you do good. When you do good, you get paid good. When you get paid good, you *be* good. And when you be good, you have it ALL good! In order to do good, you must feel good inside.

All the "goods" are connected, just as the Hi5 values all feed each other. If your precious self feels good along with your Hi5, you will live in true freedom, able to make a great contribution to the world, and for sure you will prosper.

My mission is for you to live in your Hi5. Don't waste time. Like "Ocean Wolf," live with true passion for what is most important to you, and you will live without regrets. Do it now—life is precious, and none of us know how much time we have on this earth. What's next in your life? What's your next sail?

These days, mentor, life coach and certified public speaker Zaida Garcia is busy fundraising for and creating affirming, fun events for His House Orphanage and Seeds of the Future Foundation, which provides support to children and women in distress and on the road to self-sustainability. Zaida has worked on her own to help the needy in Honduras, Nicaragua, Argentina, Tanzania, Ghana and Nigeria, and worked alongside Food for the Poor, Nourish the Children and Peace Leaders. Her dream is to create a self-sustaining village for orphans and homeless mothers with children. She created the Hi5 Workbook and the Hi5 Million Dollar Club in order to help others have a life of success and the ability to create wealth. A percentage of all revenues from her website, www.Hi5MillionDollarClub.com, will be contributed to causes addressing the needs of children and women in distress.

Janet Palmer

To Live Is To Act

I knew something was wrong when I found the discoloration on my left breast. For months I'd felt something foreign in my body, and I just wasn't up to my old self. My husband Reese was at work when I got the call to come back into the doctor's office. They'd found a lump about the size of a walnut and biopsied it—the diagnosis was breast cancer.

Until I heard those words, the possibility hadn't quite felt real. Until they were spoken, I had avoided the truth about my health. Now I was crushed.

When Reese came home, I told him the news. He wrapped his arms around me and said, "Don't worry—we'll deal with it. You'll be fine." He held me as I cried.

Chemotherapy treatments started right away, twice a week. Three weeks after the diagnosis, I rolled out of bed one morning and into the shower. Suddenly there was hair everywhere, all over my body, and I couldn't get it off. It was coming off my head in clumps. I screamed, and the tears came—but Reese and I were then primary caregivers for my mom, who had Alzheimer's, and I had to regain my composure quickly to avoid sending her into a panic. I wrapped my head in a towel, and later my nephew came and shaved my head for me on the back porch while we told jokes. I saved a little bit of my hair in a locket. I had all these plans, for six

Saturdays and a Sunday, and having cancer wasn't one of them. I had too many people counting on me.

One morning a couple of months later, my brother called at around six a.m. as I waited for my mom's day caregiver to arrive so I could be off to work at the office. "What are you doing at home?" he asked. "Reese must not have been hurt too bad. We were under the impression he was on his way to the hospital."

"What are you talking about?" I asked. I felt him freeze on the other end of the line.

"You don't know."

I felt my heart stop. "Know what?"

"Reese was in an accident at work. We were just calling to see how you are."

We hung up, and I immediately called the plant. At six in the morning, I was lost in the automated phone system, but I kept punching buttons until I got a live voice. That voice connected me with the plant's safety manager. The only thing he could tell me was that Reese was en route to the hospital; he didn't even know which one. The crash cart couldn't be accessed, and the helicopters were grounded because of weather. That meant the only option had been to wait for the ambulance, which was twenty-two minutes away from the plant. Numbly, I called the ambulance district, trying to find out where Reese had been taken.

The ambulance dispatch told me EMTs had already taken Reese to a triage room. He had suffered a traumatic head injury, and on the way to the hospital, they'd lost him three times. They were waiting for me at the hospital to sign papers so they could begin surgery.

Always the person to handle crisis in my family, I had developed a kind of crisis routine. But this was so far out of my scope I didn't know what to do—I didn't even know if Reese was alive or dead. As I drove, I prayed, "God, if it's that bad, take him home and I'll deal with the grief. But God, if there's any chance, can we please just have a miracle? Let him live—and let him have his life back." I prayed that for fifty miles.

When I walked into the hospital room, a whole team of doctors and nurses crowded around Reese, and he was in a coma. I couldn't talk to him; I couldn't ask him what he wanted me to do. All I could do was stand there in shock, holding his bloody belongings in my hands, and wait for the doctors to tell me what they were going to do. With my eyes sunk all the way to the back of my skull and a scarf wrapped around my head, it was obvious to the doctors that I was not well. Not only were they scared to death that Reese wasn't going to make it, they were scared to tell me how critical Reese was for fear of how I would take it.

Reese was rushed into surgery with a traumatic brain injury (TBI). The injury, I now understand, was to his cerebellum, his thalamus and hypothalamus. Those areas control your body temperature, your blood sugars, your heart rate, your breathing

> In the weeks that followed, every single person who approached me asked the same first question: "Do you and your husband have an advanced directive?"

and almost every other critical faculty for survival. Out of surgery, Reese was barely hanging on. His heart rate was high, he was running an extremely high temperature and he could not breathe on his own. He could go at any moment. Now it was a matter of waiting.

In the weeks that followed, every single person who approached me asked the same first question: "Do you and your husband have an advanced directive?"

The answer, then, was no. I didn't even know what that was. Even after my cancer diagnosis, Reese and I had never just sat down and said to each other, "If you got hit by the proverbial freight train today, what would your plan be? How would you want me to deal with your life?"

Nine days into the coma, the only thing Reese responded to was painful stimuli—needles stuck into his hands and feet. His fevers and the swelling in his brain continued. A trauma doctor came into the room, casually leaned against the counter and announced, "We need to do some general housekeeping."

"Excuse me?" I asked. I couldn't tell by his manner if he meant discussing something important about Reese or if he was asking me to leave the room to make way for the cleaning crew.

"You have some hard decisions to make," the doctor said. "Your husband is in a coma. His response to painful stimuli has decreased greatly. His breathing is based only on the ventilator, and we believe the damage done to his brain would not allow him

> I was standing there still thinking, Any time now he's going to wake up and want a hamburger and fries. I couldn't accept where we were—I just kept waiting for that miracle.

to breathe very long on his own. So you need to decide what you want to do. We can unplug the machines and see how he does, or for long-term care...."

The doctor kept talking, but all I heard was the word, "unplug." I asked him to explain it again.

"We would need to put a feeding tube in Reese's stomach, perform a tracheotomy to help him breathe and put a filter in his groin to prevent blood clots."

I was standing there still thinking, Any *time now he's going to wake up and want a hamburger and fries.* I couldn't accept where we were—I just kept waiting for that miracle. I said, "Are you absolutely sure this is long-term? Has he made any signs of movement at all?" I had been there twenty-four-seven, but I was desperate.

A nurse turned to me and said, "What you see is what you get."

The doctor then said, "After making your decision, should you decide to keep him on life support there are some documents you will need to sign."

"Where's the paper?" I said. "Let me sign it." I didn't even think about unplugging those machines.

My marriage to Reese was my second. My first marriage had ended badly and I spent thirteen years alone before meeting Reese. At the time of the accident, we had been married only seven years. I was bound and determined he wouldn't die on me. Still, I doubted myself.

I never knew if I made the right decisions—nobody was home inside Reese to ask. Our total stay in therapy was two hundred and ten days. I never left his side at the hospital except twice a week, when Reese's mom or another family member came in and took my place while I went for chemo. If he woke up, I didn't want him

> Call a family meeting, get out
> the notepad and say, "I love you,
> and I love you enough that I want to know
> what to do for you if something happens.
> We have to plan for our futures
> regardless of what they are."

to be alone and afraid. When I came back, I vegged on the couch, talking to him, and we'd be sick together.

I did what's called "coma therapy:" constantly talking to him, playing music, rubbing his hands and feet and reading to him, mostly from motivational books and books about TBI. I did everything I could do to stimulate his mind and body, willing him to wake up. I banned anyone from saying anything negative in the room.

Then, one day, he moved his leg. His first voluntary movement in twenty-six days. I cried! I finally knew he was really in there, and I knew I would do whatever it took to get him out. He was going home with me.

People in comas don't just wake up. Sometimes it takes months for them to fully regain consciousness, and that's how Reese was. After a while, he could blink once for "yes" and twice for "no." His therapists cried when he looked at me and spoke his first words in forty-one days: "My angel."

Under my senior picture from high school was a statement chosen by my classmates: "To live is not merely to breathe, but to act." That's what we need to do—we have to take action around our lives and the lives of our loved ones. We're so busy being busy that we don't take quality family time to really get to know the people who share our lives. One of the things I ask my family members to do now—it doesn't matter how old they are—is to write out a plan, a kind of advanced directive, so that if something were to happen, things would be taken care of for them. It's amazing what you learn when you do something like that.

Call a family meeting, get out the notepad and say, "I love you, and I love you enough that I want to know what to do for you if something happens. We have to plan for our futures regardless of what they are."

Those freight-train questions are tough ones to ask. But without the answers, you don't always make the best decisions for your loved ones—or yourself. With Reese, I knew what my heart wanted me to do, but my head didn't know if it was right. The uncertainty, the fear of the unknown, was terrible. As women, we're nurturers. We're meant to gather, nest and protect everybody. My mom always had a saying: My dad was the head of the house, but she was the neck—and she turned the head whichever way it needed to go. Some things are out of our control, though, and we can only do our best to prepare for them.

If you find yourself in a situation like mine, take great care of yourself. You can't possibly care for someone else if you can't take care of yourself. Stay in a good frame of mind. And get educated. Become an expert in your field very quickly, because you may be called upon to make decisions about your loved one's life.

Eighteen months after the accident, when Reese and I returned to the hospital to thank its wonderful staff, they didn't even recognize us. I'd put on weight and had hair—and Reese was on his feet! These days I'm still on cancer meds, and Reese continues to make progress at turtle speed. He walks with a cane and struggles to maintain balance. He can't lift his left arm; he has lost his peripheral vision and can no longer drive. Sometimes he has syncopial episodes that cause him to pass out. But he's also started school at a local college, and his first semester's grades were straight A's. Life *does* go on.

Since Reese's accident, Janet Palmer has become a full-time caregiver, speaker and TBI advocate. She has received the Missouri Governor's Volunteering with Excellence Award and has just accepted a nomination to be on the Education and Advocacy Board for the Missouri chapter of the Brain Injury Association. Visit her website, www.JanetMPalmer. com, for a free downloadable form for an advanced directive.

Taylore B. Sinclaire

Beauty, Oneness and Human Harmony

Following 9/11, I heard a story about a little five year-old boy who was trying to figure out what had happened on that day. "Why did they do it?" he asked his parents. They didn't know what to say. "We're good people," the boy continued. "How could they do it?"

His parents replied, "Well, they just don't know who we are."

"So why don't we just tell them our names?" he asked.

When I heard that, my whole body went still in recognition. I wept. That is how we reach peace: by showing each other who we truly are.

Every child is born in divine perfection, alive with her own personal essence and innate beauty. We see it in her the moment she comes into the world, fully present, full of joy and wonder. As she gets older, she learns to cloak her unique essence to make herself seem more lovable and acceptable to the world—not realizing that by doing so, she actually blocks herself from connecting with others and automatically ends up believing *I'm not enough.*

Human beings mistreat each other based on misunderstandings. When we interact and are hidden behind our constructed personalities, we can't see each other for who we truly are, in our divine perfection. As a result, we tend to mistrust and misunderstand each other; often this leads to problems as small as ugly interpersonal behavior at the office and as large as wars between nations.

But it doesn't have to be that way. When we meet in our authentic selves—showing each other our spirits, our souls—we come together naturally and in harmony. We come together in peace. When we look at true beauty that is a reflection of a person's unique, inner perfection, we feel unconditional love. I am inviting all women to step up into this realm of beauty and appreciation for our innate gifts. Women are naturally geared this way, and it's time for us to embrace this aspect of ourselves and stop apologizing for wanting to see and feel beauty.

Two decades ago, I had the privilege of discovering a science I call The Science of Human Harmony™, a discovery which put

> *Women are naturally geared this way, and it's time for us to embrace this aspect of ourselves and stop apologizing for wanting to see and feel beauty.*

me on the path of up-leveling as many people as possible into the innate perfection of their inner essence.

Through all my experiences and education in art, design, psychology and philosophy, and careers in advertising, fashion, interior design and image consulting, I learned an important fact: Our external image often has nothing to do with who we really are on the inside.

My first breakthrough came when I noticed that, even when designs were being tested on models of the same size, basic features and coloring, the same article of clothing looked completely different on each woman. I was fascinated. I finally realized it had to be the *model,* not the clothes. But what was it about *them* that was different? It was this nagging question that moved me to take the first step toward developing the art and science of harmonizing individuals' unique natural (and biologically measurable) radiance with the radiance of style, design, texture and color—the art and science of helping people find and express their authentic selves through fashion.

At first, I spent years as an image industry expert teaching color, facial shapes and body types. However, I found that none of these approaches was the answer. They are actually misleading—so seductive we are not able to actually see what we are looking at. Mainstream color-matching and facial/body matching theories cannot accurately profile people because they only deal with the surface: hair, eye and skin color; bone structure; and basic physical attributes.

Intuitively, I knew something was missing, so I continued to search for a way to accurately identify a person's innate style and inner core characteristics—her essence.

More than twenty-five years of research and experience working with and helping transform the lives of over six-thousand clients have now been developed into a system I call *IlluminEssensce®*—because it *illuminates* one's inner being. Each person has fixed

> *Have you ever felt invisible? Chances are, you were—because your outer appearance did not match up with your inner Essensce. In order to express your authentic self, your qualities have to show on the outside, too.*

sets of inner and outer core traits—a dominant energetic pattern that makes up her deepest Essensce and accurately represents the *entire* cellular vibration of a human being. Once people can find their Essensce, and dress in harmony with it, their lives change completely.

Like so many women, I once worried about dressing in a way that showed me to be grounded, competent and professional. But through the technology I discovered, I realized that I have the innate characteristics of light-heartedness and spontaneity. I was told that being grounded and serious was more important—well, the truth is *my* feet are on the ground when they're in the air! What I used to see as a fault is actually my gift and my great contribution. The same is true for you.

Have you ever felt invisible? Chances are, you were—because your outer appearance did not match up with your inner Essensce. In order to express your authentic self, your qualities have to show

> *The unique energetic pattern you transmit is reflected back to you by the people and experiences in your life.*

on the outside, too. Years ago, I would not have imagined that dressing in clothing that conveys a light and airy feeling would make people trust my natural authority. However, I now know that I disappeared completely in their eyes when I tried to be more serious or regimented, by wearing angular clothing in dark colors for example, a timeworn strategy for success in business. People doubted me and treated me *less* seriously back then, because at a visceral, subconscious level they knew my appearance was not congruent with the real me.

When you're wearing your Essensce, it opens up your field to authenticity, and you seem very credible. Sometimes it feels like a bit of a cosmic joke that we use fashion to achieve wholeness and true beauty, but the results never cease to astonish. When you are able to match your appearance with your inner Essensce, you become the most beautiful, authentic and empowered version of yourself you can be. Life opens up.

A client I began working with four years ago, a judge, says what fascinates her most is that people cannot lie to her the way they did before, now that she is wearing her Essensce. What makes the difference is letting her Essensce show through with a bit of scarf or collar peeking up over her black judge's robe, and keeping everything—even the shape of her glasses, makeup and hair—aligned with her true vibration. That is beauty in action in the world.

The unique energetic pattern you transmit is reflected back to you by the people and experiences in your life. We are all beautiful when we step into harmony with ourselves, when we sing the song we were born to sing. When you step into your Essensce, it supports you in expressing your inner truth in everything you wear *and do.* It brings you first to One—yourself—and then from One to Oneness, into harmony with other people and humanity as a whole.

Now is the time to take off your cloak of invisibility, to stand up and stand out. It is possible for you to step into harmony with your true Self, the one you were born with, and project your transcendent truth and beauty into your own life and into the world.

Now is the time to speak your true name out loud, with every aspect of your being. Meet the world in your Essensce—peace begins with you.

As the creator of IlluminEssensce®, Taylore B. Sinclaire is the originator of The Science of Human Harmony™, as well as the leading expert in non-verbal communication, fashion psychology, personal energetics, color and color psychology. She is a visionary, inspirational speaker, author, businesswoman and inventor who holds a U.S. patent on her work. IlluminEssensce® is a tool for self-remembering and self-actualization through fashion and beauty. It helps women step into the most authentic, beautiful, centered, empowered and radiant Self they have ever known. Explore further at www.IlluminEssensce.com.

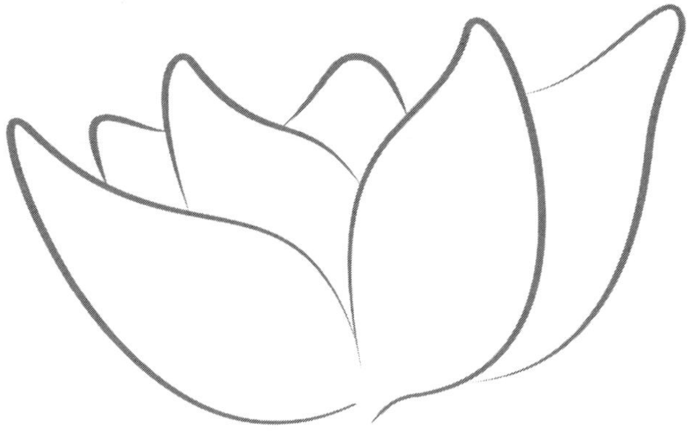

Nohra M. Leff

The Worn Coat

K enny, my eleven-year-old son, could hardly sit still as I drove. We were on our way to sign him up for Little League, his first official year in baseball. We arrived at the church auditorium, and he sprinted to the front door. Inside, kids were running all over. I walked to the sign-up table. I filled out the form and paid ten dollars, and the man in charge said, "I need another twenty-five dollars."

"For what?" I asked.

"For those," he said, pointing to a roll of raffle tickets. "You have to sell twenty-five dollars' worth."

"Fine," I said. "Give me the tickets, and I'll bring back the twenty-five dollars."

He shook his head. "Doesn't work that way."

I was heartbroken as I led my son back out to the car, and so was he. I was a single mother, and I just didn't have another twenty-five dollars. But that night taught me a crucial lesson: money talks. Oh, I know it's not original, but it felt completely original to me that night. If you don't have money, you can't compete, even in Little League baseball. You may have the best idea in the world to help someone else, but without capital, that idea is just a dream.

I decided there was only one way to get the money I needed: get a college education. My goal wasn't huge. I just wanted to support my two children in relative comfort. But when you're as cash poor as I was, that goal seemed as big as the world, and I thought I would have to overcome the whole world to achieve it.

My background: I was eleven years old when I moved from Colombia, South America, to Queens, New York. After I graduated high school in New Jersey, I married and moved to a lovely county thirty minutes north of New York City. But ten years later, I was divorced with two small children and on my own. A college education seemed like an insurmountable goal. Looking at the big picture was too much. In pursuing goals, you need to know where you want to end, but so much of the pursuit is a walk into the unknown. Keep your eyes on your feet and take one step at a time.

I enrolled at my local community college. I didn't have a lot of faith in myself, so in those early days I relied on the faith others had

> In pursuing goals, you need to know where you want to end, but so much of the pursuit is a walk into the un- known. Keep your eyes on your feet and take one step at a time.

in me, and I nurtured my relationships with those people. I kept taking little steps, and eventually all of those steps led to my goal: I earned my nursing degree. Soon after, I got a job at Montefiore Medical Center, a terrific hospital in big tough New York City and just an hour away from home.

But even though I was making good money, it still wasn't enough. When I left Colombia as a little girl, my parents gave me a brown tweed coat. It was nice, but it wasn't nearly warm enough for the brutal New York winters.

So much of life, I realized, is symbolized by that coat. You may have a coat, but it may not be sufficient to weather all of life's challenges. The only thing to do in that case is to get a better coat. I needed a better coat, and the only way I was going to get one was to continue with my education. I enrolled at Columbia University to further my career and improve my earnings by achieving a master's degree.

It's amazing what a difference one letter can make. Colombia, with an "o," the enchanted land of my youth where colorful fruits hung in the sun, and Columbia, with a "u," one of the finest universities in one of the greatest countries in the history of the world. It's a long way from that "o" to that "u."

I didn't feel I belonged at Columbia. As I walked to class on those cold January days, I was so full of doubt I'd ask myself, *Why am I doing this?* Recalling the heartbreak and humiliation of being unable to afford Little League, I remembered why. I didn't fight the

> *Whenever you're confronted by your own doubts, acknowledge them—but then tell them you don't need them, and keep moving toward your goal.*

doubts. I just pushed them into the corner, knowing they didn't serve me well. I just knew that somewhere deep inside me lay the power to define my own destiny. I would no longer be subject to the whims of external forces. I would take control. I would shape my own future. It is not our circumstances that define us; it is the way we perceive them and relate to them. Whenever you're confronted by your own doubts, acknowledge them—but then tell them you don't need them, and keep moving toward your goal.

Guess what happened? I obtained *TWO* master's degrees from Columbia, one in nursing, the second in public health. I was enormously grateful to Montefiore Medical Center, because it paid for much of my graduate school. But it wasn't just about the money. The people at Montefiore had enough faith in me that, when I was full of doubt, their vision for me supported my vision for myself. It helped me to develop very strong faith in myself and to watch my feet moving—no, racing—one step at a time.

I was finally making enough money to meet all my children's needs. My son was able to play whatever sport he wanted to play.

My daughter attended all of her proms, and she had every first-choice dress that she wanted.

Once I was able to take care of all of us, I felt a yearning to help even more people. And because of the transformation of empowerment I had experienced from having earned two master's degrees from Columbia, I felt capable of helping others beyond my immediate circle. Success breeds success, and journeys need to unfold one step at a time. If you arrive at your goal too early, you won't be ready, and you'll squander the opportunity. Trust the Universe. It knows what it's doing.

> *If you arrive at your goal too early, you won't be ready, and you'll squander the opportunity. Trust the Universe. It knows what it's doing.*

A New York law requires every woman who comes to a hospital to have had a recent breast exam and Pap smear. But many women cannot afford doctor visits for these simple procedures. I realized that if nurses were allowed to do them, they would be affordable. I took my idea to a Montefiore Vice President, and she helped me convince top management to let nurses perform the tests.

But that was just one hospital. So I wrote a proposal to send to the American Public Health Association (APHA). I wanted women to be able to obtain these tests nationwide. My superiors tweaked my proposal a bit, and submitted it, and we succeeded in having the goal adopted by the APHA. Not only that, we arranged a plan whereby resources would be allocated for women who still couldn't afford the exams.

Since then, I have achieved many successes in my field. I have coordinated large health fairs for children and families. I was invited to join the Board of Trustees of the Columbia University Nursing Alumni Association. I became Vice President of Nursing for Staff Education at another hospital. I was twice named an annual American Cancer Society "Nurse of Hope." And, I've started several businesses, one of which is geared toward helping passionate women help humanity in a larger way by going global.

Despite all of that, I still have my crises of self-confidence. Doubt still creeps up. That brown tweed coat my parents gave me? I still have it. That coat is who I am. It's a symbol of what I've become—a person who can buy better coats. But it's also a symbol of what I was and who I'll always be—an eleven year-old Colombian girl in a new country where she doesn't understand, let alone speak, the language. You cannot disown your past, and you cannot distance yourself from who you are.

But your past and who you are never need get in the way of your future and who you want to be. Instead, they can be the stepping stones by which you reach that future. So begin your journey, now. It's getting cold, and that coat in your closet just doesn't cut it anymore.

Nohra M. Leff, a proud mother and grandmother, spent twenty-seven years as a nurse at Montefiore Medical Center where she was founding director of a woman's health program. She is also the co-author of two books, and a contributor to a widely-used nursing textbook. Today, she is a successful entrepreneur with three companies: Real Hopes for Business (www.RealHopesforBusiness.com) helps small business owners grow their businesses by guiding them through the complex world of search engines and social media. Target Spanish provides targeted Spanish language education to workers in businesses, governments and non-profits. Real Hopes, LLC (www.RealHopes.com) provides solutions to people struggling to buy, sell or lease affordable homes and offers opportunities to investors to make secured real estate investments. Connect with Nohra at www.WI-REDblog.com (Women Investors-Real Estate Divas), where she inspires and empowers women to become real estate investors.

Allison Izu Song

Be Your Own Hero

What if, when you looked at yourself in the mirror, you saw the value of your own unique beauty and didn't compare yourself to other women who are taller, prettier, skinnier or smarter than you? What if you let go of the need for validation and praise from others and simply felt complete in yourself, beautiful in your own skin?

Every woman doubts her own beauty, her own gifts. If you've been waiting around for someone to rescue you or convince you that you're perfect just the way you are, you're missing your path to healing that self-doubt. Healing comes directly from you.

I'm a fashion designer. I'm short, and I'm Asian. As a young girl flipping through fashion magazines, I could never find anyone I could relate to. Shopping was a demeaning chore; nothing fit right, and every pair of pants I tried on covered my feet completely. When I looked in the mirror, I compared myself to my friends and the models I saw in magazines. I wanted to be taller, like them; I wanted larger eyes, like *her*, longer legs, like *her*. Et cetera.

When you feel small compared to everybody else, it rips away at your self-esteem, making you feel less powerful, even invisible. You might overcompensate with a big personality and strut around in four-inch heels, or you might shrink yourself to match the size you feel.

That's kind of what I did, for a while. But when I became a designer and found my own niche designing clothes for petite women, I finally really started to come into my own.

I began sewing in fifth grade, when my mom enrolled my sister and me in sewing classes. Altering my own clothes, especially hemming pants, was always a necessity. With no fashion made for women my size, I had to work with clothes to make them my own.

Although fashion was always a part of my life, I didn't realize I could do it as a career—I thought it was frivolous. I wanted to

What if you let go of the need for validation and praise from others and simply felt complete in yourself, beautiful in your own skin?

be a psychologist; I wanted to help people. Then, when I took a fashion class just for fun at the University of Hawaii, it clicked for me, and I realized that this was my passion. I decided to go for the big dream and study fashion design at the Fashion Institute of Technology in New York.

With my education as a designer, I realized quite clearly that way fashion was created for women, especially petite women needed to change. And with more research, I discovered that a petite woman was the norm because the average American woman is 5'3!" So why was the fashion industry making clothing for a 5'8" super model? I knew it was my purpose to create clothing specifically for women 5'6" and shorter; it was my purpose to make these women feel special and beautiful! Instead of continuing to feel frustrated and left out, in other words, I decided to make a place for me, and for my "vertically-challenged" sisters.

During this time, jeans were just coming back as a staple, and that seemed like a good place to start. I completely reworked basic patterns and styles to fit shorter women's proportions in both a 27" and 31" inseam. Every style accentuated their smaller frames, making them appear longer and taller.

When I met a family friend who was a manufacturer in China, I thought, *Oh my God, this is a sign!* I was thrilled to get my line off the ground so quickly. We went through the long process of sample making, fittings and production. This was my first, very expensive, lesson in becoming my own hero. When I received the shipment of twenty-one-hundred jeans, it was a complete disaster, and I wouldn't release the line to stores. I was devastated and I seriously thought about giving up. But people were counting on me and waiting for the jeans, so I had to pick myself up and move forward.

Because I grew up with an entrepreneur dad who was always ready to rescue us from our problems, I had been used to looking to others to help me fix things. Even a couple of years ago, I still dreamed that my husband would join my business, or that I could find a partner to do the dirty work and stand up to the difficult people so I wouldn't have to. I always wanted to be the nice one, liked by everybody. But faced with the need to deliver, I got my first inkling that this passive approach was not going to work. I

I decided to make a place for me, and for my "vertically-challenged" sisters.

had to rescue my line and my reputation myself. So after a healthy bout of crying and feeling sorry for myself, I went to Los Angeles and scoured the city for a manufacturer.

I soon realized that even though I was in America, I faced the same problems and issues I had in China—unethical and unreliable people. I went through three different manufacturers in Los Angeles, learning the same lesson every time: to stand up for myself, to find my inner strength. With every manufacturer, I found more of myself, more of my voice. And through it all, I managed to release three complete collections of premium petite denim.

I'm glad I didn't give up on myself or my dream when things got tough. One of the best things in the world is being at a boutique and hearing what women say when they try on Allison Izu jeans. Girls shout to their mothers from dressing rooms: "Oh my God, this NEVER happens to me! Come and look, Mom!" They're so excited to walk out of a store wearing a brand-new pair of pants that actually fit! I get emails and cards from grateful women all over the world who love knowing that someone in the fashion industry cares about them and understands their fashion needs. I realized that my instinct was correct: fashion can be transformative and healing. Learning I can save myself has had everything to do with my professional and personal growth.

When I look back at how many times I was taken advantage of in the beginning, I realize that it taught me the most valuable lesson of my life: how to come into my own strength as a woman and a businessperson—which is actually a true expression of who I am. Even now, when it comes time to deal with pushy people, I have to meditate and tell myself, *I'm a strong person! I can do this for me!* And now, I've found my perfect manufacturer, a young guy in L.A. who's like a male version of me. I might not have found him, much less known enough to appreciate him, if I hadn't been through this growth process.

I've realized throughout my growth process that it's okay to stand up for myself and ask for what I want. I grew up with the double standard: When men advocate for themselves, they're praised and admired, while women are considered "bitchy" for doing the same. I was fearful that if I spoke up for myself and commanded respect I'd be perceived as a "bitch." But I realized that it is my right to stand up and speak my mind, because who else will? I know that I'm a good, kind person, worthy of respect. Trusting in myself makes it easier to be tough when I need to be. I'm a jeans-clad "damsel *not* in distress."

I've always wanted praise and compliments—who doesn't? My husband owns his own business, too, and when he comes home I'll excitedly say, "I did this!" and, "I did that!" When he doesn't respond the way I want him to, my excitement will disappear. "Why do you feel defeated now?" he asks. "Just because I didn't react the way you wanted me to? If you're excited, stay excited!" After hearing this a few times, I realized that nobody is going to be the cheerleader I want him to be. Nobody else is going to give me the right compliment, advice or push: only I can do that for myself. I'm the only one who knows exactly what I need.

I thought, *How come I can be really supportive of all my friends, but I can't even support my own* self? Now I talk to myself as I would to a close friend, saying, *Great job!* and, *I'm so proud of you!*

Think how powerful it would be if before we went to sleep, we reviewed our day and gave ourselves props for the things we've

> *Learning I can save myself has had everything to do with my professional and personal growth.*

accomplished. It's really worked for me: Every night before I close my eyes, I review my day and say the things I would say to my best friend if she were dealing with my problems or if she had the amazing day I had.

You can do this for yourself, too! Give yourself the love and support you would give anyone else you care about, even for what seem like the smallest things: You made that phone call, even though you were afraid to. You stood up for yourself—awesome. Treat yourself to a pedicure, like you would a friend. Or simply rest and relax! It's the little things we do to take care of ourselves that keep us happy and sane.

We all look outside ourselves and think how great other people are, how much prettier, more accomplished, smarter. But we forget that no one else could do what we do, the way we do it. Once we own that, own "This is who I am," we'll stop looking for heroes and see that they live right here, within our (sometimes short) selves.

Allison Izu Song, 5'2", is a fashion designer dedicated to creating clothes specifically made for petite women. A graduate of the Fashion Institute of Technology in New York, she launched Allison Izu, an environmentally-friendly, made-in-the-USA clothing company that makes flattering and fashion-forward clothing for women 5'6" and shorter. Based in Hawaii, Allison is expanding her market to the mainland United States and Asia, and she plans to create a non-profit to help people accept and celebrate non-stereotypical beauty. Connect with Allison at www.AllisonIzu.com or shop online at www. ShopAllisonIzu.com.

Haumea Hanakahi

Phenomenal Mischief

J ust think: what could you do in this world if you felt safe, loved and supported? What phenomenal change would you create on the planet and in your own life? We were born to be phenomenal mischief-makers, helping humanity and the earth to evolve.

Many of us, especially women, are used to looking outside ourselves for a sense of safety. Everyone wants and needs love and nurturing; we tend to seek it out in male partners. Searching hard for love and security, we often meet with disappointment and end up feeling badly about ourselves. Unfortunately, this approach bypasses our true source of love, strength and nurturing. That true source, though, is never out of reach. It is available to each and every one of us, here and now, as we tap into our spirit-selves. There we find a fathomless well of strength and love, a sense of safety and wellbeing that allows us (men too) to express our feminine wisdom. Harnessing this extraordinary power, becoming the change agents we were meant to be, is our key to the creation of heaven on earth.

There is a world called "The Rainbow World" that has been present with me ever since I can remember. In this Rainbow World, everything radiates with strong, harmonious life force. I see rainbows everywhere. The trees are throbbing with rainbow colors; water vibrates with rainbows; the earth is alive! This is the world I remember—or perhaps I am remembering the future.

I would say I had a troubled childhood. I felt alone, isolated and unseen. My mother and I had a challenging relationship and were not close. The role I played in our family was of the helpful, invisible child. I was in survival mode, and it was more important for me to know and anticipate other people's needs than to try to get mine met, still less to recognize that I had any.

I survived mostly by living deep in my own remembrance of how life used to be, long before I was born—the Rainbow World of divine harmony and joyful, open connection and telepathy with others. From toddlerhood, I connected and communicated with nature, animals and unseen worlds. I could ask a question of

> We were born to be
> phenomenal mischief-makers, helping
> humanity and the earth to evolve.

the universe and it would always be answered, usually by nature. I wondered why this world wasn't as I remembered. Among humans, I was virtually mute; from the ages of six to eleven I remember lying in bed and performing a nightly ritual, counting all the words I'd said that day on one or two hands.

Because I felt so unsafe, everything was life or death to me. I related to and felt like a wild animal in the presence of danger; I was always scared, but I had to put up a brave front. I thought that if people sensed my weakness and vulnerability, they might harm or kill me. I lived in extremes and feared that if I showed who I truly was, I might bring shame and trouble upon my family—and a torturous death to myself.

It wasn't until many years later, living on a sacred mountain at a remote monastery near the Mexican border, that I began to feel safe around humans. Those I encountered on the mountain were of my "tribe," esoteric and often considered rebels by society. I felt no judgment from them. And I was ecstatic under those extraordinary stars. I hiked at night, unafraid of wild animals. I expanded spiritually. For the first time (without the use of alcohol or drugs), I felt a sense of freedom amongst other humans. Experimenting with the use of my own voice, I discovered what it was like to be me, to speak and live my truth. With that feeling of liberation came the winds of change.

With this newfound sense of strength and security, I continued, but at a deeper level, my medicine journey as a wisdom keeper and intuitive healer. Little did I know that I was about to be initiated at such a level that I would be plummeted into a healer's crisis lasting more than fifteen years: At thirty-three, I experienced a devastating, life-threatening pesticide poisoning. Almost over-night, my capacities completely changed. I had difficulty reading, math was almost impossible and I could not use the computer.

My speech slurred; memory loss was rampant; and I became so highly sensitive to chemicals that I could no longer travel freely, visit with friends or safely live in the city. I couldn't work because

> *The key is to find what our own needs are, what makes us feel good, and start taking care of ourselves rather than waiting around for someone else to do it for us.*

my functional thinking had become so limited—tests verified that I had suffered brain damage and was dealing with severe auto-immune conditions. I believed I had embodied our Mother Earth's struggle with toxic waste. And again, I thought everything was life or death. So, once again, I turned to nature for nurturance and answers.

I became so highly sensitive that my brother said I had the nose of a dog, smelling things others could not. I also felt things that others did not. Plants were grounding, life-saving. When I touched them, I knew how they would affect my body, or another's. The super-strength I discovered then—being able to look at a problem or health issue and instantly see its root cause—is the foundation of my work. It helps me to connect others with the deep, universal, feminine wisdom essential to the health and evolution of our species and planet. My sacred, silent Hawaiian name means "earth's evolution as guided and blessed by the heavens."

Developing a sense of safety, even a visceral knowing that we are loved and protected no matter what, is central to participating in this evolution—we do this by choosing to feel good. In my former way of being, as a woman, I spent so much time and energy pursuing love and security that I actually ended up completely focused on my insecurities and what I thought was *wrong with me*. I suffered greatly.

But that time of suffering is over. Having the courage and creativity to finally question unexamined assumptions that I inherited as a woman has allowed me to open myself more fully to spirit; say "YES!" to life; own my power AND playfulness; and be more spontaneous. In that grounded joy and passion, I can do the things I always wanted to do, but didn't know how to before.

Many of us women have a difficult time knowing what we need and what feeds us. We're gifted at caring for others and anticipating their needs—but our secret wish is that they fulfill *our* needs. And we resent them when they don't. I have learned that whenever I'm holding onto resentment, I'm holding onto an old, hurt and fearful identity. Essentially, I'm living in the past. But our true spirit-selves are not shadowed by hurt and fear. The key is to find what our own needs are, what makes us feel good, and start taking care of ourselves rather than waiting around for someone else to do it for us.

It's time for us to stop the blame game and truly BE our unique, juicy, powerful selves instead. Change can (but doesn't have to) be tough, and it takes at least 21 days of consistent habit-breaking practice. I couldn't afford NOT to change. And isn't that the case with you also? Together, we can be change-bringers, engaging in creative action as phenomenal mischief-makers.

I suggest you make a list right now. A list of things and activities you need to feel balanced, energized and good. Go ahead and name as many things as you can in three minutes. Look that list over daily and keep a copy nearby at all times. Add to it. And for goodness sake, do at least one of those things for yourself every day. If you're feeling down or tired, there's even more need to do something on your list. Try to have a mix of activities. Some you do by yourself, some with friends, some with family. And as radical as it may sound, how about making a new habit of feeling good— for no reason at all? As we start doing more for ourselves, we feel

> *As we start doing more for ourselves, we feel more whole and connected, more safe, secure and nurtured.*

more whole and connected, more safe, secure and nurtured. Then we can live our lives from a much fuller place, with more to give others and ourselves.

A silver-haired woman named Peace Pilgrim was one of my favorite phenomenal mischief-makers. From 1953 to 1981, she walked more than twenty-five-thousand miles around the United States, teaching and spreading the messages of peace. For these twenty-eight years she walked with only the clothes on her back, neither asking for nor accepting money.

One night, Peace Pilgrim was picked up by a trucker. As soon as she hopped into the truck, she could feel that he meant to do her harm. But she maintained with him the peacefulness and love that she knew—the source—and soon, that loving energy dominated. As they talked, the trucker was transformed. He became one of her biggest advocates, walking with her and looking out for her on the long journey for peace that did not end until her death, and which affected countless others, inspiring them to peaceful action.

Peace Pilgrim knew she was safe, because her life was centered in spirit, love and peace. This gave her true power and grace: total freedom to pursue her own authentic path. This level of joy and independence from fear is radical for a human, radical for a woman, radical for an older woman. And it is possible for each of us. She demonstrated living from the spirit, fully and with joy, feeling safe because she knew she had everything she needed and all the protection in the world. That sense of genuine, self-generated security brings great freedom and inspires beautiful, radical action.

Phenomenal mischief is what women create when we feel safe enough to follow our grandest dreams and play brilliantly. It's magic that happens when we use our gifts of receptivity and intuition. Will you answer the call?

Not long ago, while dancing (my practice and one of my greatest joys), I felt an unsafe energy and almost withdrew from the bliss I was feeling in my own movement. I prayed and heard a strong, gentle voice say, "It's okay. You can play. You can be who you are. You are safe. From now on, live all your moments as if you are safe and loved and truly embrace being ALIVE. Worry not that you may make a mistake that will harm others—who you are cannot intentionally harm others. You will always be led back to your true path." Let the phenomenal mischief begin!

Haumea Hanakahi is a visionary storyteller/speaker, entrepreneur, advisor and Renaissance woman using her gifts to help create heaven on earth by connecting people—especially women of a certain age—to the strength and feminine wisdom rising within themselves and the world. A professional PSYCH-K® and Auracles Colour therapist, she works as an intuitive with clients around the world, sharing wisdom from nature, indigenous cultures and unseen worlds. She is a powerful creatrix, helping to midwife the new Rainbow World of the ancient-future. Connect with Haumea at www.RainbowBlessings.com (for visionary entrepreneurs) and www.TheSavvySafetyNet.com (for part-time expanded income opportunities).

Dixie Daly

All You Have to Do Is Ask

A s the fifteenth of seventeen children, I may not be the most obvious poster child for "ask and you shall receive." I could have expected a life of hand-me-down adventures and secondhand dreams to go along with my older siblings' clothes and toys. But I never expected anything less than a miracle, and my whole life has shown me that "ask and you shall receive" is true.

When I was a little girl, I loved the movie *Cinderella*. My big dream was always my prince—my husband. I left home at thirteen, and moved in with my brother and his wife. I was happy there, but when I met Ed a little while later, I knew that he was my prince, and my real home was with him.

Ed was seventeen, sweet, strong and handsome, and my heart did little flips every time I saw him. I remember walking by his house and saying to myself, *I'm going to marry that guy someday.*

We became high school sweethearts. Dating at such a young age was quite an experience, with me not even knowing how to drive; but we were happy just going for a walk holding hands or going to our favorite ice cream parlor, The Purple Cow. On weekends we hiked at the national parks or had fun roller skating. Going to the movies was special—*Love Story* was one of our all time favorites.

Three years after we started dating, my brother, sister, Ed and I were in a car accident; our car was hit from the side, throwing the four of us into a tree. We were rushed to the emergency room, where my sister and I were admitted for our injuries.

Coincidentally, before us, two other girls had been admitted from another accident. As Ed nervously paced the waiting room, he overheard an emergency room doctor informing a nurse that the two girls in the car wreck had died. Sure that my sister and I had passed away, Ed panicked and stormed into my room. Overcome, Ed saw me alive and well, dropped to one knee and cried, "Dixie! I thought I lost you. I never, ever want to lose you—will you marry me?"

I burst into tears in my hospital bed. "Yes!" I said, grasping my prince's hand. "Yes. I've always known I wanted to spend my life with you."

When we got married a little while later, I was only a junior in high school. Not many would think that being married so young would work, but we knew how strong our love was, and we listened to our hearts. All this time, ever since I asked for my first big dream of love, I've had Ed's support. It has given me the faith, strength and confidence to keep on asking for what I need and want, and to go for my dreams.

Years later, after my kids were all grown up, I wanted nothing more than to start my own business. I heard about a conference for women in business in Dallas, Texas, and felt so strongly drawn I made the eighteen-hundred-mile drive with two friends. *I want this to mark a new chapter in my life,* I thought, as we sped down the highway. I showed up fresh as a daisy in Dallas, all dressed in pink, not knowing that pink would change my life forever.

The conference was amazing. Even though I had faith in "ask and you shall receive," when I heard a speaker tell a whole audience of women, "You can have whatever you want, ladies—all you have to do is say it and believe it," I flushed with excitement, and felt my whole body buzz with inspiration.

It was true, wasn't it? It had happened to me before, when I fell in love with my prince. "Okay!" I said. "Let me at it!" I made connections with tons of awesome women, all ready to support me in my new business. Everywhere I went, I asked for help and information. And my new mentors and collaborators were right there for me. Right away, I knew that a big reason I wanted to succeed was so I could give back.

When I got home, I started dreaming up and developing products. One morning, I woke up and thought, *Tickled Pink! Nobody out there has a chocolate bar called "Tickled Pink."* I got

> Once I put something out there, I own it. I have no doubt about that. I feel what I want to do next, and it happens!

on the computer and educated myself about what it takes to own a product. I taught myself about trademarks, labeling and manufacturers.

People said, "I've never made pink chocolates, but I guess I can try!" Ideas for products, even a jingle, rushed in as if they'd only just been waiting for me to ask them to show up. I was having a blast, falling in love again—this time with my own purpose in life. My business chose me—amazing!

Because I'm getting all that confidence and strength from other women and at home, Tickled Pink Boutique has exploded. I now travel many times a year to go to networking groups and share knowledge and inspiration with other women. I meet all kinds of people; I never stop coming up with ideas; and wherever I go, I put out not only what I want, but also how I can help. In return, someone always comes to me, arms stretched open wide, saying, "I will help you." I asked for a distributor, and I got one. I asked for a great marketing connection, and I ran into a QVC rep the very next day.

Once I put something out there, I *own* it. I have no doubt about that. I feel what I want to do next, and it happens! Amazing. That gift is out there for you, too. It's just important to be clear about what you want. Know the "what"—you don't have to figure out the how and the why. If you're clear about the what, the how and why will happen for you. The what is your foundation. When you ask for what you want and need, everything will flow naturally from it. You don't have to struggle.

Sometimes you need to shift gears and ask again, "What is my what?" That's a good thing. Your "what" evolves right along with *you*.

Supporting each other is the key to life. When my friend became sick without insurance, we did a fundraiser for her that ended up connecting me with someone to help market my chocolates. I had no intention of even looking for that, but my helping her helped us both.

When I needed financing, I talked to a woman in one of my networking groups.

"You know I'll help you!" she said. "All you had to do was ask!"

ASK. What would you have the courage to ask for, if you knew

> ASK. What would you have the courage to ask for, if you knew you absolutely would receive it? Well, go ahead and ask for it! Your dream is only waiting for you to speak up.

you absolutely would receive it? Well, go ahead and ask for it! Your dream is only waiting for you to speak up.

Women have an easy time giving, but not the easiest time asking or receiving. Ask and you *will* receive—if you don't ask, who do you have to blame but yourself? Your choices are yours to own. And really, all there is to receiving is saying two little words: Thank you.

Accept that receiving is just as powerful as giving. Either way, you are enjoying life, and giving joy to people around you. Let yourself trust in goodness and abundance—let yourself fall in love with possibility. The whole universe will work to make your dreams come true, as long as you do too. Tickled Pink Boutique is a gifting business, and my three words for my business are Give,

Receive and Enjoy—because when you give or receive, you truly enjoy life.

Since that conference in Dallas, I've fallen madly in love with connecting people who can help each other. It is such a natural way for women to succeed in business. I see myself now as a connector, more than just a creator or entrepreneur. Just as with my business,

> Be a good listener, especially to yourself. Your intuition will help you ask for what you want and need.

I didn't know I could really do it at first—I did it locally, involved in all the community organizing, but now I'm national, even international, with it.

When I wake up in the morning, I ask myself, *who needs me today? Who can I support today?* Get your marketing hat on and connect with your soul-mates through social media. Some will become your teammates, some your lifelong friends. Just get out there and ask! Exactly the right person will show up with what you need next. It's thrilling, seeing what magic people can make with each other.

We have an average of forty-thousand thoughts a day. Your intuition will make some of them stand out more than others. I believe that God gives ten people an idea, but the one who acts on it owns it. The one who asks will be heard. So have faith in your dream, be positive and make it happen. Believe in yourself. Give, receive, enjoy—that's what it's all about. All you have to do is ask. Be a good listener, especially to yourself. Your intuition will help you ask for what you want and need.

My handsome prince Ed and I are closer and more in love than ever. This June, we celebrated thirty-seven wonderful years of marriage, together with our seven beautiful grandchildren and our four loving children (who have all married their high school sweethearts as well, and all live within ten miles of our house). If we hadn't followed our hearts and asked for what we wanted all those years ago, I wonder where we would be today. It wasn't just the hand of fate that brought us together—we *asked* for the love we've got.

Our dreams and aspirations are like our childhood sweethearts; the purest and most beautiful parts of us, the great loves of our lives. We need only ask to spend the rest of our days with them and they will come and live with us always. Live life to the fullest by living in the moment—all you have to do is ask!

Wearing her signature pink, Dixie Daly is a great cheerleader to have on your side. The founder and CEO of Tickled Pink Boutique, Dixie combines her entrepreneurial energy with a lifelong passion for helping others, and generously shares her expertise and extensive network of contacts to encourage other businesswomen and unite them to gather in the presence of inspiration. Dixie designates a portion of all the Boutique's sales for conference scholarships and donations to nonprofits. She was the International Business Matchmaker of the Year in 2006, and is the recipient of a Prestige Award. She is currently writing a book, and has written a "Pink" jingle, "Let's Pink The World," which now is a cell phone ringtone on iTunes. Connect with Dixie at www.TickledPinkBoutique.com.

Join Us!

As we come to a close, return to the first chapter, written by Dr. Jean Shinoda Bolen, and ask yourself, "What is my assignment?" After reading the stories in this book, what will you take on? What will you allow to grow and give rise to all of the possibilities? How will you aid in the building of a thriving world?

Whatever your assignment is, I hope that you view life as a treasure hunt. On the hunt you will be tested by twists, obstacles, foreign lands and new languages, but you will also encounter the assistance of unseen helpful forces.

Your resolve will surprise you, as will the guidance and assistance from people who are genuinely interested in creating with you. Through the power of prayer, you will discover a strength you never realized you had and beauty in unexpected places and wastelands ready to be turned into fields of riches. And the treasure you will surely find? It is the fulfillment of your destiny, your heart's desire, your calling—and you are a gift to the world.

From my heart to your heart, this is my wish for you:

That you will take up your assignment (either with renewed enthusiasm, or for the first time). That you will seek not the adoration of others, or pay heed to the critical nature of others, but instead stand firm in your own truth. That you will live up to your own standards and forgive yourself when you can't. That you will listen to your own counsel, first and last. That you will remember love: Love in your essence, love of self, love of others and from others and love of that unseen nature that so brilliantly sustains you. And that you will be a leader to yourself *first*—if you do, self-respect and grace will surely follow.

> *And the treasure you will surely find? It is the fulfillment of your destiny, your heart's desire, your calling—and you are a gift to the world.*

I invite you to come join us at GetYourWomanOn.com and dive into your adventure, and to let us help you on your journey. Come and meet like-minded and like-hearted women who are here to help each other and lend a hand to those who need it.

Do you want to have the ability to live in your full essence, your breathtaking beauty, elegant grace and your undeniable power? This is your path to experiencing the rewards of financial success Take my hand and we will do this together.

Remember that you, my precious sister, you as you are now, are more than enough. Your assets are bigger than the balance sheet of the richest nation, deeper than the deepest ocean, more expansive than the vast, unseen galaxies, more nourishing than the purest water sources. You, who juggle all that you have on your plate while supporting others—you are more valuable than all the gold in the world.

Embarking on your treasure hunt is a yummy, fun, exhilarating, hilarious, eyes-wide-open right of passage that I hope you will begin today.

I know what I'm creating next. Do you?

We invite you to experience the *Get Your Woman On* MULTIMEDIA book.

Now that you've been inspired by these remarkable women, you can learn more from the online version of GET YOUR WOMAN ON on your computer or iPad in an exciting, next-generation multimedia format.

Through AUDIO and VIDEO conversations that supplement the text, the co-authors share more knowledge and encouragement to help you experience the joys of your own woman power.

We offer you a GIFT of several chapters from the *Get Your Woman On* multimedia book at:

www.GetYourWomanOnBook.com

If you wish to buy the complete multimedia book, please use this coupon code to receive a substantial discount.

Coupon Code — Book7

We also invite you to share your thoughts about our books with our community on our Facebook page at:

www.YinspireMediaFacebook.com

We welcome you to experience Yinspire Media bestselling books, in both print and multimedia editions. Enjoy several free chapters of each multimedia book. If you buy a complete multimedia book, use the coupon codes to receive a substantial discount. You can purchase the print versions of these books at Amazon.com

Fight For Your Dreams
The Power of Never Giving Up
www.Fight4YourDreams.com
Coupon Code – Book6

Living Proof
Celebrating the Gifts that Came Wrapped in Sandpaper
www.LivingProofMBook.com
Coupon Code – Book5

How Did You Do That!
Stories of Going for IT
www.HowDidUDoThat.com
Coupon Code – Book2

The Law of Business Attraction
Secrets of Cooperative Success
www.LawOfBusinessAttraction.com
Coupon Code – Book1

Transforming Through 2012
Leading Perspectives on the New Global Paradigm
www.2012MultimediaEbook.com
Coupon Code – Book 4

The Wealth Garden
The New Dynamics of Wealth Creation in a Fast-Changing Global Economy
www.WealthGardenBook.com
Coupon Code – Book 3